The Supply and Demand Paradox

For permission to reuse copyrighted content from *The Supply and Demand Paradox—A Treatise on Economics*, please contact:

Copyright Clearance Center
222 Rosewood Drive
Danvers, MA 01923
USA
Telephone: 978-750-8400
Fax: 978-646-8600
www.copyright.com

Copyright Clearance Center is a not-for-profit organization that provides copyright licensing on behalf of Byron Fisher.

Library of Congress Control Number: 2007905312
Publisher: BookSurge, LLC
North Charleston, South Carolina

Visit www.TheSupplyAndDemandParadox.com
or
www.amazon.com to order additional copies.

The Supply and Demand Paradox
A Treatise on Economics

Byron Fisher

2007

The Supply and Demand Paradox

TABLE OF CONTENTS

Acknowledgments

I would first like to thank my family. Gratitude is also extended to the staff and faculty of my alma mater, Richmond—The American International University in London as well as all the staff of the American Institute for Foreign Study. I wish to thank The Fund for American Studies for affording me the opportunity to spend a semester in Washington, D.C., where I studied at Georgetown University and participated in an internship on Capitol Hill. I wish to extend a special thanks to Professor Thomas C. Rustici, who serves as a faculty member with The Fund for American Studies. He is the first economist with whom I shared my theory pertaining to *The Supply and Demand Paradox*. He subsequently showed me how my theory could be used to illustrate the process by which laws are created and repealed (i.e., *The Market for Laws*). Last but not least, I would like to give a heartfelt thank you to all the brave men and women currently serving in the U.S. Armed Forces.

To Economic Thought

I.

INTRODUCTION

Will a consumer demand a good or service simply because a producer supplies it? Will a producer supply a good or service simply because a consumer demands it? These are two questions to consider when attempting to understand how markets work. The best approach to take when answering these questions is to analyze the rational motivations of both producers and consumers. Consumers demand and consume goods and services while producers produce and supply goods and services. Consumers typically demand the goods and services that satisfy their needs and wants. Producers are able to satisfy their needs and wants with the compensation they receive for addressing the demands of consumers. Consumers are not likely, however, to demand a good or service simply because a producer supplies it to them because no incentive exists for them to do so. An incentive does exist, however, for a producer to supply a good or service simply because consumers demand it. For example, consumers are not going to purchase apples from a fruit stand just because the fruit stand owner is selling them. They may purchase apples because they are hungry, but they will not purchase apples just because someone is selling them. On the other hand, a fruit stand owner will sell apples just because consumers demand them. This theory is entitled the Supply and Demand Paradox. While common interpretation would lead one to believe that *Supply* and *Demand* are separate and equal components of market activity, they are, in fact, separate and unequal market forces. By focusing specifically on responses to market activity, one should be able to determine that *Demand* is stronger than *Supply*. The reason is that there is an incentive to address the demands of consumers, whatever they may be. When taking into account the role of incentives in a market, one should be able to derive the following sequence of causality: *Supply* does not cause *Demand*, but *Demand* causes *Supply*. I will introduce a counterfactual model in the following section in order to provide a more tangible illustration of this sequence of causality. The Supply and Demand Paradox is a far cry from the *Field of Dreams* notion of "If you build it, they will come." On the contrary, building (supplying) a baseball diamond will not result in someone demanding it because no incentive exists for an individual (or group of baseball players, for that matter) to demand a baseball field simply because someone supplied it. A more plausible sequence of causality would be "We want it, so build it!" The purpose of this book is to explore the possible applications of the Supply and Demand Paradox. This theory will make it possible to apply economic processes to the non-traditional market for laws and evolution while applying it to traditional, yet illegal, markets such as the market for contract killers (hitmen). To achieve this, however, requires a clearly stated theorem and use of a counterfactual model. Making tangible the role of incentives in this theory as well as establishing rules for applying the counterfactual model will also be necessary. It is also important to point out that applying the counterfactual model to real-world scenarios will be a very complex process that will require both partial and full applications of the model. In the broadest sense, this theory must be applied to scenarios where the good or service being demanded already exists in the market in some way, shape, or form. There are only specific exceptions to this, which I will explore later.

II.

OUTLINE OF THE GENERAL THEORY

A. Research Questions
- Will a consumer demand a good or service simply because a producer supplies it?
- Will a producer supply a good or service simply because a consumer demands it?

B. Theoretical Approach to the Research Questions

In a free market, the act of supplying a good or service will not result in a demand for it. However, if a consumer demands a good or service, someone will always supply it. There is no incentive for a consumer to demand a good or service simply because a producer supplies it. There is an incentive, however, for a producer to supply a good or service simply because a consumer demands it. This theory is entitled the Supply and Demand Paradox (SDP).

C. The Supply and Demand Paradox (SDP)— Theorem

The act of supplying a good or service will not result in a demand for it, whereas the act of demanding a good or service will result in it being supplied.[1]

D. The Supply and Demand Paradox (SDP)—Model

(1a)

Supply ≠ Demand		S ≠ D
	or	
Demand = Supply		D = S

Where:
Supply (S) = the act of supplying a good or service
Demand (D) = the act of demanding a good or service

The SDP Model is comprised of two separate, yet equal elements:

(1b)

$$S \neq D—Supply\ Side$$

$$D = S—Demand\ Side$$

III.

THEORETICAL CONSIDERATIONS

A. The SDP Theorem and the Role of Incentives

Incentive Matrix	
1	Incentive
0	No Incentive

SDP	Incentive Factor
Demanding a good or service simply because a producer supplies it	0
Supplying a good or service simply because consumers demand it	1

B. The Law of Demand Conservation

Like Energy, Demand cannot be created or destroyed; it can only change from one form to another.

IV.

RULES OF APPLICATION

1. Disequilibrium in the *Supply Side* of the SDP Model can result from either no demand (D = o) or demand that is represented by a numerical value less than that of the supply (S > D). Thus, S ≠ D if o ≤ D < S. *Example: 100 apples can be supplied in a market (S =100) where none of the apples is consumed (D = o / S > D) or 99 of the apples are consumed (D = 99 / S >D).*

2. Equilibrium in the *Demand Side* of the SDP Model can be achieved if demand is represented by a numerical value of at least one and supply is represented by a numerical value greater than or equal to that of demand. Thus, D = S if D ≥ 1 and S ≥ D. *Example: 1 consumer may demand a clock (D = 1), while between 1 and 5 producers may attempt to supply it (S = 1 or S = 5 / S ≥ D).*

3. We can apply the SDP Model in scenarios where the variables represent proportions of a given population. In such a scenario, disequilibrium in the *Supply Side* of the SDP Model can result from a good or service being supplied by a statistical majority (S ≥ 51%) that is demanded by a statistical minority (D ≤ 49%). Thus, S ≠ D if o% ≤ D < S. Also, equilibrium in the *Demand Side* of the SDP Model can be achieved if a good or service is demanded by a statistical majority (D

$\geq 51\%$) and is supplied by any given percentage of the population. Thus, $D = S$ if $D \geq 51\%$ and $0\% < S \leq 100\%$. *Example: See The Market for Laws.*

4. We can apply the SDP Model in scenarios where the variables DO NOT represent numerical values. Therefore, disequilibrium in the *Supply Side* of the SDP Model can result if the act of supplying a good or service does not cause a demand for that good or service. Equilibrium in the *Demand Side* of the SDP Model may be achieved in such a scenario if the act of demanding a good or service causes it to be supplied.

5. Apply the SDP Model with the assumption that only rational goods or services are being considered. *Example: No one has ever supplied the Fountain of Youth, despite centuries of continuous demand.*

6. We can apply the SDP Model in scenarios involving irrational goods or services, only when the demand for an irrational good or service results in its eventual supply. *Example: For centuries, people both demanded and considered irrational a manned mission to the moon until NASA supplied a successful moon landing in 1969.*

7. Depending on the specific application, disequilibrium in the *Supply Side* of the SDP Model can result in the generation of a subsequent demand. *Note: This rule does not contradict the Law of Demand Conservation because the concept of Demand generation as it applies to this rule simply indicates that a new form of a previously existing Demand has emerged.*

8. We can apply the SDP Model by using homogeneous variables (similar variables for both the *Sup-*

ply and *Demand Sides* of the SDP Model) or het-erogeneous variables (different variables for both the *Supply* and *Demand Sides* of the SDP Model). *Note: I established this rule in respect to Rule of Application (7).*

9. We must apply the SDP Model with the assumption that all prices relating to market transactions originating on the *Supply Side* are non-negotiable and that all prices relating to market transactions originating on the *Demand Side* are negotiable. *Example: A consumer will not demand a good or service simply because a producer supplies it, even if a producer agrees to supply the good or service to the consumer free. However, a producer will supply a good or service to a consumer just because the consumer is demanding it once they agree on a price for that good or service.*

10. In respect to the *Law of Demand Conservation*: *Demand* can change forms spontaneously. There is no predetermined length of time that *Demand* can remain in any one form. Also, *Demand* may become segmented, in which case the various segments can change forms independently.

V.

EXAMPLES AND APPLICATIONS

A. The Market for Laws

This section focuses on applying the concepts of the Supply and Demand Paradox to the *Market for Laws*, or the process by which laws are created and repealed. After considering the concepts of the Supply and Demand Paradox and their application to the *Market for Laws*, one should be able to appreciate that the act of supplying a specific law will not result in a demand for it. Likewise, one should also be able to internalize that demanding a law will result in its supply. The 18th Amendment to the U.S. Constitution, the 21st Amendment to the U.S. Constitution, and the USA PATRIOT Act are the laws I will address in this section in order to illustrate how the Supply and Demand Paradox relates to the *Market for Laws*.

The SDP and the 18th & 21st Amendments to the U.S. Constitution

During Prohibition in the United States (US), the manufacture, sale, or transportation of alcoholic beverages became illegal with the ratification of the 18th Amendment to the U.S. Constitution. However, many continued to consume and distribute alcohol, despite the legal infringements. A law that citizens do not abide by indicates that the law is something that the citizens do not want. Despite the demand, it took thirteen years to repeal Prohibition.

In this case, a law was supplied to a group that did not demand it. In other words, the act of supplying this particular law did not result in a demand for it. However, the act of demanding a law repealing the 18th Amendment resulted in the ratification of the 21st Amendment.

Background

"[Alcohol] became an American problem between 1790 and 1830, during the expansive years of the early republic."[2] The consumption of alcohol, which was a previously accepted custom, had begun (in 1790) to be viewed as a hindrance to society's progress.[3] "Organized efforts to promote temperance appeared in the 1820s as part of the extraordinary outburst of reform activism that transformed the United States in the first half of the nineteenth century."[4] Reform activism continued to grow well into the 20th century. During the early 1900s, "[t]he confidence of American dry activists was bolstered by a parallel stream of anti-liquor policies enacted by other nations."[5] Also, national organizations at the helm of the temperance movement such as the Women's Christian Temperance Union (WCTU / nationalized in 1874) and the Anti-Saloon League (ASL / nationalized in 1896) began to make their voices heard in Washington. In December of 1913, "'Grand committees' from the ASL and the WCTU joined other temperance workers, many of them grey veterans of dry agitation, in a parade of four thousand marchers down Pennsylvania Avenue to the Capitol."[6] After they reached the Capitol, the ASL and WCTU presented a Prohibition resolution "to Democratic [S]enator Morris Sheppard of Texas and Congressman Richmond P. Hobson of Alabama, a naval hero from the Spanish-American War and an outspoken foe of 'the great destroyer' alcohol. The two men [subsequently] agreed to introduce the measure in their respective chambers."[7] The actions taken by the Anti-Saloon League and the WCTU on that day set in motion the events that would lead to the ratification of the 18th Amendment to the Constitution. Organizations that were leading the fight in the temperance movement had officially passed the buck to the federal government. The following year, Congress made one failed attempt at amending the Constitution in favor of prohibiting alcohol. However, interest for national Prohibition remained intact within the Congress. The Congress, therefore, sought to attempt again to implement Prohibition at the start of Word War I. After the United States entered World War I in April of 1917, subsequent wartime patriotism "significantly aided [in] the swift adoption of prohibition. The pressures of wartime patriotism discredited and silenced German brewers and the beer supporters, who had been among the most effective opponents of the dry advance."[8] On August 1, 1917, only four months after the United States entered World War I, the U.S. Senate approved, by a vote of 65-20, a proposal for a constitutional amendment prohibiting the production and distribution of alcohol within the United States. On December 18, 1917, the U.S. House of Representatives also approved a proposal for a constitutional amendment prohibiting the production and distribution of alcohol within the United States by a vote of 282-128. The proposal for this constitutional amendment then went to the states for ratification. Mississippi became the first state to ratify this proposal in January of 1918 while Nebraska was the thirty-sixth to ratify it in January of the following year. The 18th Amendment then became part of the Constitution and took effect one year after the states approved it. The amendment reads:

AMENDMENT XVIII

Section 1.

After one year from the ratification of this article the manufacture, sale, or transportation of intoxicating liquors within, the importation thereof into, or the exportation thereof from the United States and all territory subject to the jurisdiction thereof for beverage purposes is hereby prohibited.

Section 2.

The Congress and the several States shall have concurrent power to enforce this article by appropriate legislation.

Section 3.

This article shall be inoperative unless it shall have been ratified as an amendment to the Constitution by the legislatures of the several States, as provided in the Constitution, within seven years from the date of the submission hereof to the States by the Congress.[9]

Once the 18th Amendment took effect, a very interesting chapter in American history emerged. "The unwillingness of many Americans, especially in cities, to obey [the 18th Amendment] which had been passed over their protest created a market for smugglers and bootleggers."[10] Americans, despite a tangible barrier called the 18th Amendment, consumed alcohol during the Prohibition era. "On college campuses, polls revealed, two of three students drank alcoholic beverages during prohibition."[11] The Prohibition Bureau, created to enforce the measures put forth in the 18th Amendment and initially placed under the control of the commissioner of the Internal Revenue Service, was anything but helpful in combating the trafficking of illegal alcohol into American cities. "During the first six years of prohibition, one of every twelve [Prohibition] Bureau agents was fired for taking bribes, issuing illegal permits, conspiring to sell illegal liquor, or other corrupt acts."[12] The corruption apparently was shared with other law enforcement organizations because "[i]n one federal courthouse during one month in 1925, fifty-eight policemen and prohibition agents were convicted of conspiring to break the prohibition laws."[13] Around that same time, organizations, such as the Association Against the Prohibition Amendment (AAPA), began to take action in response to the public outcry for the repeal of Prohibition. Even though the AAPA was founded in 1918, two years before Prohibition took effect, it had at that time successfully acquired a political role similar to the role held by the ASL and WCTU in the years leading up to the ratification of the 18th Amendment. The AAPA successfully infiltrated the Democratic National Committee in 1928 and spent the following four years molding the party's agenda into one that favored repealing the 18th Amendment.[14] This left (then) New York State Governor Franklin D. Roosevelt no choice but to adopt a position in favor of repealing the 18th Amendment in order to secure the Democratic Party's nomination for the 1932 presidential election.[15] Roosevelt went on to win the 1932 election, defeating incumbent Hoover by over seven million votes.[16] "Before the new administration took office, Congress passed a repeal amendment specifying that special state conventions, not sitting legislatures, ratify the amendment, thus assuring popular control of the repeal process."[17] By February of 1933, a proposal for an amendment to repeal Prohibition had been approved by both the U.S. Senate (63-23) and the U.S. House of Representatives (289-121). The proposed amendment then went to each state's convention. "Repeal of the 18th Amendment became official on December 5, 1933, after the Utah convention became the thirty-sixth state gathering to ratify the 21st Amendment."[18] The amendment reads:

AMENDMENT XXI

Section 1.

The eighteenth article of amendment to the Constitution of the United States is hereby repealed.

Section 2.

The transportation or importation into any State, Territory, or possession of the United States for delivery or use therein of intoxicating liquors, in violation of the laws thereof, is hereby prohibited.

Section 3.

This article shall be inoperative unless it shall have been ratified as an amendment to the Constitution by conventions in the several States, as provided in the Constitution, within seven years from the date of the submission hereof to the States by the Congress.[19]

Analysis

The 18th Amendment to the Constitution prohibited the manufacture, sale, or transportation of alcoholic beverages within the United States. In order for the 18th Amendment, and any constitutional amendment for that matter, to go into effect, the Congress, by a two-thirds majority in both houses, had to propose an amendment that two-thirds of the states subsequently approved (either by the state legislature or a special state convention). The United States is a modern republic and, in theory, each elected representative shares the values of his or her constituents. The federal government and each state government do not always win an election by a statistical majority (51%). However, they collectively represent the majority of the U.S. population. Therefore, one should assume that the motivations of the politicians responsible for approving the 18th Amendment to the Constitution mirrored those of their constituents. Based on observations of political activity at that time, it can be said that the majority of the U.S. population initially supported the 18th Amendment to the Constitution. The majority of politicians at the state and federal levels demanded a constitutional amendment prohibiting alcohol production and consumption. These politicians, therefore, had an incentive to supply themselves and the whole of the nation with a constitutional amendment prohibiting alcohol in various capacities.

Therefore:

(2a)   D18th Amendment = S18th Amendment

Where:
D18th Amendment = the act of American Politicians demanding a constitutional amendment that would prohibit alcohol within the United States / the act of American Politicians demanding the 18th Amendment to the U.S. Constitution

S18th Amendment = the act of American Politicians ratifying, and supplying the United States with, a constitutional amendment prohibiting alcohol within the United States / the act of American Politicians ratifying and supplying the United States with the 18th Amendment to the U.S. Constitution

While the act of American politicians demanding a constitutional amendment to prohibit alcohol resulted in one being supplied, supplying U.S. citizens with the 18th Amendment to the Constitution did not result in it being demanded. During the thirteen years that the 18th Amendment was enforced, many U.S. citizens continued to consume and/or aid in the supplying of alcoholic beverages. This included the politicians responsible for approving the 18th Amendment as well as the law enforcement officials responsible for enforcing the 18th Amendment. Many federal agents and other law enforcement officials who were responsible for enforcing the 18th Amendment took bribes from suppliers of alcohol, thus aiding in the supply of an illegal good. These actions indicated that a large percentage, if not the majority of, the U.S. population did not demand the constitutional amendment that was being supplied to them.

Therefore:

(2b)   S18th Amendment ≠ D18th Amendment

Where:
S18th Amendment = the act of American Politicians ratifying, and supplying the United States with, the 18th Amendment to the U.S. Constitution
D18th Amendment = the act of American Politicians and the majority of the U.S. population demanding the 18th Amendment to the U.S. Constitution

The fact that a large percentage[20] of the U.S. population did not abide by the 18th Amendment to the U.S. Constitution indicated that the U.S. population had a subsequent demand for a constitutional amendment repealing the measures put forth in the 18th Amendment. Supplying the American population with a law they did not demand resulted in the generation of a demand for the law to be repealed.

Therefore:

(2c)   (S18th Amendment ≠ D18th Amendment) = DR/21st

Where:
(S18th Amendment ≠ D18th Amendment) = the U.S. population's disproportionate demand for the 18th Amendment to the U.S. Constitution
DR/21st = demand among the U.S. population to repeal the 18th Amendment to the U.S. Constitution / demand among the U.S. population to ratify the 21st Amendment to the U.S. Constitution

And

(2d)   DR/21st > D18th Amendment

Where:
DR/21st = demand among the U.S. population to repeal the 18th Amendment to the U.S. Constitution / demand among the U.S. population to ratify the 21st Amendment to the U.S. Constitution
D18th Amendment = demand among the U.S. population for the 18th Amendment to the U.S. Constitution

Note: DR/21st represents a new form of a previously exist-
ing Demand. Americans have always demanded the ability to
shape their government through democratic processes. Therefore,
the demand among Americans to retain the ability to democrati-
cally control their government changed forms to a more specific
form, which was the demand for the 18th *Amendment to the U.S.*
Constitution to be repealed (DR/21st) (see The Law of Demand
Conservation).

The measures put forth in the 18th Amendment to the
U.S. Constitution were repealed by the 21st Amendment.
The demand for repeal of Prohibition resulted in American Politicians approving and subsequently supplying a
constitutional amendment doing just that.

Therefore:

(2e)   DR/21st = SR/21st

Where:
DR/21st = the act of the majority of the U.S. population
demanding a constitutional amendment repealing the
18th Amendment to the U.S. Constitution / the act of the
majority of the U.S. population demanding the ratification
of the 21st Amendment to the U.S. Constitution
SR/21st = the act of American Politicians supplying
a constitutional amendment that repealed the 18th
Amendment to the U.S. Constitution / the act of American
Politicians ratifying the 21st Amendment to the U.S.
Constitution

The act of supplying the 18th Amendment to the U.S.
Constitution did not result in a demand for it. However,

the act of the majority of the U.S. population demanding that the U.S. Constitution be amended in favor of repealing Prohibition resulted in the 21st Amendment to the U.S. Constitution being ratified.

The SDP and the USA PATRIOT Act

After the terrorist attacks of September 11, 2001, there was an immediate demand to improve Counterterrorism (CT) capabilities within the United States. A bill was then introduced to Congress for the USA PATRIOT Act, which met little, if any, resistance. The act of demanding a law will result in it being supplied almost immediately.

Background

The Uniting and Strengthening America by Providing Appropriate Tools Required to Intercept and Obstruct Terrorism Act of 2001(USA PATRIOT Act / H.R. 3162) was introduced to the U.S. House of Representatives on October 23, 2001, by Congressman F. James Sensenbrenner, Jr., of Wisconsin's 9th Congressional District. Within twenty-four hours, the U.S. House of Representatives had approved it by a vote of 357-66. The following day, the U.S. Senate approved the USA PATRIOT Act by a vote 98-1. On October 26, 2001, President George W. Bush signed the USA PATRIOT Act into law (Public Law No: 107-56). This occurred only three days after Congressman Sensenbrenner introduced the USA PATRIOT Act to the U.S. House of Representatives.

Analysis

Congress demanded improved CT capabilities in the wake of the September 11th attacks, as did the majority of the U.S. population. The USA PATRIOT Act was not passed on the basis of a referendum (meaning citizens did not vote for it at the polls). However, the United States is a modern republic. This means that people elect members of Congress on the basis that those members will vote in their favor for initiatives such as the USA PATRIOT Act. Therefore, one should not consider any polls measuring the public's opinion regarding this matter and should assume that the demand for the USA PATRIOT Act (circa 2001) in Congress mirrored the demand among the U.S. population at the time. With that said, it is important to note that the USA PATRIOT Act passed in the U.S. House of Representatives with 84% of the membership present approving the Act, and it passed the U.S. Senate with 98% of the senators present approving the Act.

Therefore:

(3a) $$DPA = SPA$$

Where:
DPA = the act of the U.S. Congress demanding improved CT capabilities in the wake of the September 11th terrorist attacks / the act of the U.S. Congress demanding the USA PATRIOT Act

SPA = the act of the U.S. Congress approving (supplying) the USA PATRIOT Act

The U.S. Congress approved (supplied) an improved CT capability (the USA PATRIOT Act) in the wake of the September 11th terrorist attacks simply because it was being demanded (demanded among members of the U.S. Congress as well as the American Public). However, the

U.S. Congress has never demanded the USA PATRIOT Act simply because it was being supplied.

Therefore:

(3b) $SPA \neq DPA$

Where:
SPA = the act of the U.S. Congress approving (supplying) the USA PATRIOT Act
DPA = the act of the U.S. Congress demanding the USA PATRIOT Act

The U.S. Congress has never had an incentive to demand the USA PATRIOT Act simply because it was being supplied. This is most evident when one considers the turmoil among members of the U.S. Congress when the USA PATRIOT Act was facing expiration in late 2005. A substantial number of the senators and congressmen who initially voted for the USA PATRIOT Act were opposed to its renewal.

B. From Fish to Frog

Many theories suggest that amphibians, such as frogs, evolved from fish. There were, and still are, many barriers in place that would make it extremely difficult for a fish to make the transition from an underwater habitat to a land-based habitat. For example, fish have fins. Fins are not intended for walking, only swimming. In order for a fish to survive on land, it would need feet. Fish also have gills. Gills allow fish to filter and absorb the water's oxygen content. In order for a fish to make a successful transition to land, it would need lungs in order to inhale atmospheric oxygen (O_2) and to exhale carbon dioxide (CO_2). The SDP Model will be applied to this scenario in order to provide a tangible analysis of how an extraordinary evolutionary process such as this one took place.

Background

Approximately 570 million years ago, vertebrate animals (animals with backbones) began to evolve into a variety of fishlike animals. Two hundred million years later, these fish-like animals inhabited lakes, rivers, lagoons, and estuaries. During the later part of the Devonian period, these fishlike animals began to develop limbs with digits, such as fingers and toes. The fishlike animals that developed limbs with digits are known as tetrapods.[21] A tetrapod is any vertebrate animal that has four legs or any vertebrate animal that is a descendant of an animal with four legs. Tetrapods, over the course of a 350-million-year period, left their aquatic environment behind in order to continue life on land. The modern descendents of these tetrapods include amphibians such as frogs and salamanders and amniotes such as mammals, turtles, and crocodiles.[22] "Tetrapods belong to a once large and well-populated group of vertebrates known as the sarcopterygians, or Sarcopterygii."[23] Sarcopterygians are more commonly known as lobe-finned fish.[24]

Many of the theories regarding tetrapod evolution deal directly with the environment in which the tetrapods lived during the Devonian period.

> [In] the early years of the 20th Century, [an] observation was made that sediments from the Late Devonian period, the time when tetrapods were assumed to have evolved, consisted largely of red-beds.[25] These are layers of sandstone that often have a reddish color due to the presence of iron, and such sediments are found all over the world from this period. The eastern United States, northern and eastern Europe, Australia, and China all have them. They have usually been interpreted as the result of arid or semiarid conditions.[26]

In respect to the belief that arid conditions existed during the late Devonian period, scientists have considered the following theories regarding tetrapod evolution:

Theory 1

> [A]rid conditions caused a general drying up of the pools and lakes in which the lobe-finned ancestors of tetrapods lived, leaving the creatures stranded. The suggestion was that [the lobe-finned fish] that had lungs and were able to breathe air were the most likely to have been able to survive.[27]

Theory 2
After the drying up of the pools and lakes,

> those fishes whose fins were strongest and most resembled the structure of limbs, such as the lobed fins of *Sauripteris* or *Eusthenopteron*, were favored by a strong selective pressure on the animals to get back into the water. Those with more limblike legs were better able to struggle over the dry surface and so were more likely to reach another pool. According to this idea, limbs actually arose to enable the animals to get back into water, not to be better able to leave it.[28]

Theory 3
In respect to an observation made of modern amphibians, it is believed that tetrapods did not develop limbs for walking.

> Looking at modern amphibians gave one worker the idea that limbs might originally not have been for walking at all. Rather than walking away from drying pools, many modern amphibians, and indeed crocodiles as well, bury themselves in the mud at the bottom of the pool, where they stay until the rains come again. It was therefore suggested that the limbs of early "prototetrapods" might have been evolved for burrowing into the mud.[29]

Theory 4
In respect to another observation made of modern amphibians:

> [M]ost modern amphibians, rather than seeking new pools when their own dries up,

congregate in the drying pools and often die there. If they are disturbed for any reason, they may leave the pool, but the directions they take are random.[30] Some may find new pools, but the selective pressure would be on those that could best withstand desiccation, not those with the strongest legs. The same would have been true [during] the Devonian [period]. Population pressure in existing pools today may sometimes stimulate migrations in humid conditions, and in this case, the selective pressure may have been to favor those with limbs.[31]

Theory 5

"It was suggested that the animals laid their eggs in shallow water that then dried up, and the conditions favored those that could survive in temporary pools."[32]

Theory 6

"[T]etrapods, either the adults, their eggs, or their young, were being pressured by predatory fish or arthropods to seek more and more marginal habitats where the predators could not follow."[33]

Theory 7

During the Devonian [period], increase[s] in [the] diversity of fishes in the water occurred at the same time as the radiation of plants onto land, followed by an increase in the variety and numbers of arthropods that fed on them. By the Late Devonian [period], vegetation at the margins of lakes and rivers was dense and lush, with the appearance of forests whose structure resembled that of modern forests. The many arthropods living in and on this vegetation would have provided a rich and unexploited resource for any vertebrate that could reach them. No competing vertebrate forms were on the land before them, so that any vertebrate that could in any degree survive out of, or partially out of, water would find itself at an advantage, independent of what predation pressures might have existed in the water.[34]

These seven theories deal exclusively with tetrapods gaining the ability to walk. However, while the ability to walk is something that tetrapods gained for themselves, the ability to breathe is something that they acquired from their aquatic ancestors. Theories relating to the tetrapods' ability to breathe stem from observations made of modern fish. The *Lepisosteus* and *Amia* are two fish that possess both lungs and gills. When these fish are in low-temperature waters, they rely on their gills to obtain the oxygen content that they need. However, when the water temperature rises, the oxygen content in the water becomes depleted. Consequently, the *Lepisosteus* and *Amia* become dependent on their lungs so that they may acquire oxygen from above the water's surface. Observations of this process have shown that oxygen obtained by the *Lepisosteus* and *Amia* through breathing with their lungs increases by 50% in warm waters.[35] It is for these reasons that scientists believe that tetrapods evolved in warm waters.

Some suggest that all bony fish of the Devonian era had an all-purpose gas bladder. Some fish of this era used their gas bladder to control buoyancy (gas bladder used for buoyancy control = swim bladder), while others used it as a lung.[36] Fossil evidence suggests that the lungfish, an ancestor of the tetrapod, was the first fish to obtain oxygen from above the water's surface.[37] Based on the observations of the *Lepisosteus* and *Amia*, the lungfish more than likely needed to acquire oxygen from above the water's surface because a rise in the temperature had depleted the oxygen content in the water that they inhabited.[38] Observations of modern lungfish have shown that the lungs of the lungfish serve the same purpose as the swim bladders did for the bony fish of the Devonian era (e.g., air breathing and buoyancy control).[39] Therefore, it is safe to say that the lungs of the lungfish are its "swim bladder." This, of course, does not indicate any spontaneous development of lungs in this species of fish or any other for that matter since we assume all bony fish of the Devonian era had a swim bladder. What the fossil evidence of the lungfish does indicate, however, is how lungfish may have developed an alternate use for a swim bladder. This is assuming that lungfish used swim bladders only to control buoyancy. Also, even if swim bladders could easily be converted for breathing purposes, fossil evidence clearly indicates how other physical changes occurred in lungfish over time that allowed them to breathe in a manner that would enable them to take in air from above the water's surface.[40] Modern "[lungfish] have a very specialized method of inhaling air by gulping it from the surface of the water. It involves the use of a 'cranial rib' unique to lungfishes and a highly modified shoulder girdle that swings round beneath the chin as the buccal cavity expands."[41] Changes to the mouth and palate, as based on comparisons of lungfish fossils and modern lungfish, "may be associated with the unique way in which they form a seal as the gulped air is swallowed, rather than with the requirements of a crushing dentition."[42] According to fossil evidence, the earliest lungfish did not have any of these physical characteristics.[43] This means that "surface breathing" is a capability that lungfish gradually acquired over time. Scientific evidence clearly identifies the lungfish as a tetrapod ancestor.[44] Therefore, the ability to breathe atmospheric oxygen was likely to have been present in the tetrapod lineage long before tetrapods began to make the transition toward land.

Analysis

To clearly illustrate the factors that caused fish to evolve into amphibians, the SDP Theorem will first be applied broadly to this specific theory of evolution. This requires an examination of the cumulative effect of a water-based species attempting to make the transition to a land-based habitat. This will allow for the establishment of a clear pattern of causality in the evolutionary process. While the process of evolution that resulted in a fish evolving into amphibians took several million years, it is easy to identify a sequence of causality by examining in a collective manner the motives of each species in the evolutionary chain. The transition from water to land depended on several actions made by several different species in the evolutionary chain. Therefore, we can successfully extrapolate a sequence of causality in evolutionary patterns by designating all species in the evolutionary chain as one general species. For the purpose of this analysis, we will designate as Fish X the species in the evolutionary chain between and including fish and amphibians.

Fish X = [Coelacanths + Lungfish / Porolepiforms + Tetrapods (includes amphibians)]

Any creature that has both the exclusive physical ability to survive in an underwater habitat and the desire to live in a land-based habitat faces a dilemma. Fish X's aggressive efforts to breathe atmospheric oxygen and to walk on land indicated that it had a desire to live on land. However, Fish X had physical qualities that allowed it to live only in an underwater habitat. The fact that Fish X wanted to make the transition to a land-based habitat meant that Fish X had a subsequent desire to obtain the physical characteristics that would have allowed it to survive on land. Fish X, therefore, had ceased to demand the physical form that "nature" had supplied. No incentive existed for Fish X to demand a particular physical form simply because "nature" was supplying it.

Therefore:

(4a) $$SA \neq DA$$

Where:
SA = the act of "nature" supplying Fish X with *Physical Form Alpha*
DA = the act of Fish X demanding *Physical Form Alpha*

And

Physical Form Alpha = the physical form that allowed Fish X to live in a water-based habitat (its traditional physical form)
Physical Form Bravo = the physical form that would allow Fish X to survive in a land-based habitat

Fish X was still living in an underwater habitat when it made the decision to make the transition to a land-based habitat. Thus, it continued to demand *Physical Form Alpha* to some degree. However, Fish X's ultimate goal was to make a transition to a land-based habitat.

Therefore:

(4b) $DB > DA$

Where:
DA = Fish X's demand for *Physical Form Alpha*
DB = Fish X's demand for *Physical Form Bravo*

Disequilibrium in the *Supply Side* of the SDP Model (4a) resulted in a corresponding demand for *Physical Form Bravo* being generated.

Therefore:

(4c) $(SA \neq DA) = DB$

Where:
$(SA \neq DA)$ = Fish X's disproportionate demand for the physical form that "nature" initially supplied (*Physical Form Alpha*)
(DB) = the act of Fish X demanding a physical form that would allow it to survive on land (*Physical Form Bravo*)

Note: DB represents a new form of a previously existing Demand. Fish X always demanded a physical form that would allow it to survive. It is just that Fish X's demand for the ability to survive changed forms from a demand for the ability to survive in an underwater habitat to a demand for the ability to survive in a land-based habitat. Therefore, Fish X's demand for Physical Form Bravo (DB) is an alternate and more specific form of Fish

X's demand for the ability to survive (see The Law of Demand Conservation).

Fish X's demand for a physical form that would allow it to survive on land caused "nature" to supply Fish X with a physical form that allowed it to survive on land (*Physical Form Bravo*).

Therefore:

(4d) $DB = SB$

Where:
DB = the act of Fish X demanding a physical form that would allow it to survive on land (*Physical Form Bravo*)
SB = the act of "nature" supplying Fish X with a physical form that allowed it to survive on land (*Physical Form Bravo*)

Physical Form Bravo did not materialize all at once. It was comprised of several distinct and separate physical changes separated by substantial lengths of time. In order to gain insight into the evolutionary process, we must apply the SDP Model to specific developmental stages. While there were many stages to the evolutionary process involving amphibians, fish gaining the ability to breathe atmospheric oxygen and walk on land are arguably the most extraordinary. Therefore, we will now apply the SDP Model individually to each of these developmental processes.

Fish Gaining the Ability to Breathe
The ability to breathe atmospheric oxygen (O_2) is a fundamental characteristic shared by all land vertebrates. This

ability is something that the lungfish of the Devonian period (Devonian lungfish), which inhabited bodies of water that were lacking in oxygen content, needed greatly. Fish typically possess gills, which allow them to filter and absorb the oxygen content in the water. The Devonian lungfish needed to seek alternate means at gaining the oxygen content that they needed. The only alternative for the Devonian lungfish was to obtain oxygen from above the water's surface. One of the main problems with doing this, however, is that the oxygen above the water's surface is of an atmospheric quality. This type of oxygen can be absorbed only through lungs. The Devonian lungfish had gills, which were not intended for breathing surface air. Nevertheless, the Devonian lungfish were desperate for alternate sources of oxygen and attempted to breathe surface air. The Devonian lungfish subsequently abandoned use (primary usage) of their gills in order to accomplish alternate breathing methods. The fact that the Devonian lungfish were not using their gills for breathing purposes meant that they were not demanding the gills that "nature" was supplying.

Note: According to fossil evidence, only the earliest lungfish lacked the ability to breathe surface air. Thus, for the purposes of this analysis, one should consider only such lungfish. For the purposes of this analysis, we will (collectively) designate such lungfish as Lungfish X.

Therefore:

(4e)   SGills $\neq$ DGills

Where:

SGills = the act of "nature" supplying the Lungfish X with gills

DGills = the act of the Lungfish X demanding gills

It is also important to note that just because Lungfish X was attempting to breathe atmospheric oxygen while it had only functional use of its gills did not mean that it ceased demanding its gills. What it does indicate, however, is that Lungfish X's demand for a physical form that would allow it to breathe atmospheric oxygen exceeded its demand for gills. For the specific purposes of this analysis, we will designate as Physical Form X the physical form that allowed Lungfish X to breathe atmospheric oxygen.

Therefore:

(4f) $\qquad$ DPhysical Form X > DGills

Where:

DPhysical Form X = Lungfish X's demand for a physical form that would allow it to breathe atmospheric oxygen

DGills = Lungfish X's demand for gills

Disequilibrium in the *Supply Side* of the SDP Model (4e) resulted in the generation of a corresponding demand for Physical Form X.

Therefore:

(4g) $\qquad$ (SGills $\neq$ DGills) = DPhysical Form X

Where:

(SGills ≠ DGills) = Lungfish X's disproportionate demand for its gills

DPhysical Form X = Lungfish X's demand for a physical form that would allow it to breathe atmospheric oxygen / Lungfish X's demand for Physical Form X

Note: DPhysical Form X represents a new form of a previously existing Demand. Lungfish X always demanded the ability to acquire the oxygen content that it needed. Lungfish X's demand for the ability to acquire the oxygen content that it required simply changed forms from a demand for the ability to maintain primary functional use of its gills to a demand for the ability to convert its swim bladder into a functioning lung (see The Law of Demand Conservation).

Lungfish X's demand for the ability to acquire oxygen content could no longer be facilitated by its gills (primarily), but by another one of its physical characteristics. Lungfish X already possessed a swim bladder that it could easily convert into a functioning lung. Lungfish X also required certain other physical alterations to occur (which were described previously) in order to achieve the ability to breathe surface air. It is important to note, though, that Physical Form X collectively represents the conversion of Lungfish X's swim bladder into a functioning lung as well as the other physical alterations that Lungfish X needed to occur in order to gain the ability to breathe atmospheric oxygen. The act of Lungfish X demanding a physical form that would allow it to breathe atmospheric oxygen caused "nature" to supply Lungfish X with Physical Form X.

Therefore:

(4h)   DPhysical Form X = SPhysical Form X

Where:

DPhysical Form X = the act of Lungfish X demanding the ability to breathe atmospheric oxygen / the act of Lungfish X demanding Physical Form X

SPhysical Form X = the act of "nature" supplying Lungfish X with the ability to breathe atmospheric oxygen / the act of "nature" supplying Lungfish X with Physical Form X

Tetrapods Acquiring the Ability to Walk

The tetrapods that sought to make the transition from a water-based habitat to a land-based habitat had to mimic certain characteristics of a land-based species in order to survive on land. They mimicked the ability to walk since they had already acquired the ability to breathe atmospheric oxygen in a previous evolutionary process. Tetrapods initially attempted to walk with their fins. However, as stated previously, fins are intended only for swimming, not walking. Tetrapods needed feet in order to sustain locomotion by walking. The fact that they made several attempts to walk while they still possessed fins indicated that they were subsequently demanding feet. Thus, from the first instance a tetrapod attempted to walk with its fins, "nature" was supplying it with fins that it no longer demanded.

Therefore:

(4i)   SFins ≠ DFins

Where:

SFins = the act of "nature" supplying tetrapods with a particular physical form (fins)

DFins = tetrapods' demand for the physical form that was being supplied to it by "nature" / tetrapods' demand for fins

Tetrapods were still living underwater after they made their first attempt to walk. Thus, they were still demanding fins to some extent because they continued to use them on a day-to-day basis. However, tetrapods' primary goal was to walk on land.

Therefore:

(4j) $DFeet > DFins$

Where:
DFeet = tetrapods' demand for "nature" to supply them with a physical form that would allow them to walk / tetrapods' demand for feet
DFins = tetrapods' demand for the physical form being supplied to them by "nature" / tetrapods' demand for fins

The fact that tetrapods continuously attempted to walk with their fins indicated that tetrapods' overall demand for feet exceeded their demand for fins. Tetrapods' desire to walk with their fins generated a demand for feet.

Therefore:

(4k) $(SFins \neq DFins) = DFeet$

Where:
$(SFins \neq DFins)$ = tetrapods' disproportionate demand for the physical form that was being supplied to them by

"nature" at the time / tetrapods' lack of demand for their fins

DFeet = tetrapods' demand for "nature" to supply them with a physical form that would allow them to walk on land / tetrapods' demand for feet

Note: DFeet represents a new form of a previously existing Demand. Tetrapods always demanded the ability to stay mobile. With the changing environment, their fins could no longer facilitate their demand to stay mobile and they would require certain subsequent physical alterations to occur. Therefore, Tetrapods' demand for the ability to stay mobile would change forms from a demand for the ability to use their fins to a demand for feet (see The Law of Demand Conservation).

Tetrapods' demand for "nature" to supply them with a physical form that would allow them to walk on land resulted in "nature" eventually supplying tetrapods with feet.

Therefore:

(4l)   DFeet = SFeet

Where:
DFeet = the act of tetrapods demanding a physical form that would allow them to walk on land / the act of tetrapods demanding feet

SFeet = the act of "nature" supplying tetrapods with feet

The act of "nature" supplying tetrapods with fins did not generate a corresponding demand for fins because no incentive existed for the tetrapods to demand their fins simply because "nature" was supplying them. The demand among tetrapods to acquire the ability to walk resulted in "nature" supplying them with feet because an incentive existed for "nature" to supply tetrapods with feet simply because they were demanding them. The incentive that "nature" received for supplying tetrapods with feet related to the ability to maintain a balance of life in the ecosystem despite drastic environmental changes.

C. Evolution of the Coffeehouse

We can trace the origins of some of the world's largest financial markets to the coffeehouses of 18th century London and New York. Organizations such as the London Stock Exchange, the New York Stock Exchange, and Lloyd's of London all began in the grandest of coffeehouses. One should consider why financial markets were present in coffeehouses in the first place and why they are not located within the same coffeehouses today.

Background

The Royal Exchange in 17th century London was a diverse center of commerce. Merchants and traders from around the world conducted business in the exchange's large courtyard.[45] Businesses located in the streets and alleys leading to the Royal Exchange benefited from the large volume of traders traveling to and from the exchange.[46] Exchange Alley opened in 1662 so that businesses could benefit from the high volume of merchants near the Royal Exchange.[47] The primary objective of Exchange Alley's developers was to build coffeehouses.[48] These coffeehouses, however, were not to resemble traditional coffeehouses, but coffeehouses that catered to the type of businessmen who frequented Exchange Alley. The first coffeehouse branded in such a fashion was referred to as "the new [coffeehouse] in Exchange Alley."[49]

"[T]he new [coffeehouse] in Exchange Alley"[50] was located on the southern side of Exchange Alley. This particular coffeehouse sought to appeal to the businessmen of Exchange Alley by offering free coffee.[51] This notion suggested, ironically, that the primary interests of the coffeehouse owner did not relate to selling coffee. By January 8, 1663, "the new [coffeehouse] in Exchange Alley"[52] had become a "venue for auctions of imported cloth [that were] sold 'by an inch of candle.'"[53] (Bidding for auctions conducted "by an inch of candle" began when a section of a wax candle was lit and ended when the flame went out, with the final bidder acquiring the good being auctioned.[54]) Soon afterward, a man by the name of "Walter Elford, a girdler, [was] granted a lease for 'the Coffee-house scituate in Exchange Alley' on 27 May 1664 at an extraordinarily high price, paying a premium of [200 pounds sterling] and a rent of [100 pounds sterling] per annum for twenty-one years."[55]

Elford's Coffee-House differed from its predecessors insofar as it was one of the first grand coffeehouses in London. Previous coffeehouses, more modestly constructed, operated on a much smaller scale. Elford's Coffee-House further encouraged a connection with the Royal Exchange by evolving into a marketplace of its own. Elford's Coffee-House burned down in the Great Fire of 1666.[56] Thomas Garraway, a man who had previously managed a coffee-house in Sweetings Rents, began where Elford had left off by subsequently acquiring his lease and building a coffee-house of his own in Exchange Alley.[57] Thomas Garraway's Coffee-House in Exchange Alley was similar in scale to that of Elford's Coffee-House. Strategically placed on a very visible corner, it was highly accessible to the traders and merchants passing through Exchange Alley.[58]

By the end of the 17th century, London newspapers were regularly advertising auctions in coffeehouses. "Advertisements announced the goods to be sold and, as the coffeehouse was the location only of the auction itself, in which warehouse they could be viewed."[59] Not long thereafter, the new coffeehouses had also begun "to develop specialist news services for financial information. In 1692, John Houghton reported that merchants in Garraway's Coffee-House could consult a list which displayed 'what Prices the Actions bear of most Companies trading in Joynt-Stocks.'"[60]

Another publication that was of interest to merchants of this era was the *Marine List*. The *Marine List* "reported the arrival and departure of ships at English and foreign ports."[61] Edward Lloyd established the first *Marine List* in 1692. Lloyd acquired the information that he used in his *Marine List* from the merchants in his coffeehouse, which was located on Lombard Street in London.[62] While auctions were also held in Lloyd's Coffee-House, it was the publication of his *Marine List*, as well as other financial publications, that made his "coffee-house the centre of the London shipping world."[63] The wealth of shipping intelligence produced within Lloyd's Coffee-House resulted in it becoming the headquarters of the marine insurance business.[64] Both "underwriters who accepted the risks and the intermediaries, [who were] known as office-keepers"[65] called Lloyd's Coffee-House home during this period. While the "new coffeehouses" were diversifying around this period by providing financial information, they also began to move away from the practice of auctions as well.

Businessmen conducted auctions in coffeehouses based on the notion that all participating parties could bid for securities. Now, auctions had been deemed beneficial for those vendors who could successfully identify a buyer for what they were selling. However, auctions did not afford buyers the opportunity to present their terms to the vendor.[66] "Another solution was intermediation, [which consisted of] using individuals who were entrusted with the task of finding buyers or sellers on behalf of clients who wished to dispose of or purchase securities. These men were known as brokers."[67] By the early part of the 18th century, a vast array of businessmen, who fulfilled the roles of stockbrokers, frequented the coffeehouses of Exchange Alley.[68] Furthermore, "[specialized] dealers—who became known as jobbers—bought and sold securities on their own account."[69] These "jobbers" engineered their own markets "by facilitating buying and selling, because if someone wanted to sell, jobbers ensured they could always find a buyer."[70] Jonathan's Coffee-House, a coffeehouse located in Exchange Alley, was a regular haven for these "jobbers."[71]

Merchants and traders appeared to have tolerated the role that coffeehouses played in the financial market all the way up until the mid-18th century. It was during the mid-18th century (circa 1750) that the stockbrokers of Jonathan's Coffee-House began to display their disdain for the environment that the coffeehouse fostered. The proprietorship of the coffeehouse did not discriminate among the public as to who could gain entry. Thus, the stockbrokers felt that they lacked privacy when conducting business within the coffeehouse.[72] "In 1761, 150 brokers joined together [...] to exclude the casual interlopers and made an agreement with the proprietor for the exclusive use of the coffee room for three hours a day for [1200 pounds sterling] per annum, during which time the coffee room would be open only to members paying an annual subscription of [8 pounds sterling]."[73]

After facing intense opposition for their actions, the stockbrokers agreed to leave Jonathan's Coffee-House and acquired a separate venue in which to conduct their trading. They succeeded in obtaining a lease for a site near

Sweetings Alley and Threadneedle Street. The building that the stockbrokers eventually moved into was completed in 1773.[74] "The three-storey neoclassical building, initially called New Jonathan's but soon renamed the Stock Exchange, contained the dealing room in a large high-ceilinged room on the ground floor, with a coffee room on the floor above."[75] "As before, the brokers paid 6 pence a day (or [7 pounds sterling and 80 pence] per annum) to gain access to the room; but in 1801 a committee of proprietors succeeded in closing the room to all but those who had been accepted as members and paid a subscription."[76] The actions taken by the stockbrokers who had previously occupied Jonathan's Coffee-House were repeated by the businessmen who called Lloyd's Coffee-House home.

During the 1760s, the underwriters and intermediaries who frequented Lloyd's Coffee-House allowed their dissatisfaction to tangibly manifest itself for how the (then) proprietor of Lloyd's Coffee-House, Thomas Lawrence, managed the coffeehouse. By 1769, a committee of these underwriters and intermediaries came to an agreement to disembark from Lloyd's Coffee-House and founded a coffeehouse of their own in Pope's Head Alley, which was known as New Lloyd's. The businessmen who founded New Lloyd's Coffee-House decided to establish some rather unique ground rules. Since the shipping news being relayed in their coffeehouse was so valuable, they decided that, just like New Jonathan's, entrance to New Lloyd's would be made available only to businessmen who had acquired a membership and had made subsequent required payments.[77]

Financial markets within the United States also emerged from coffeehouses. During the colonial era, coffeehouses in both New York and Boston held regularly scheduled auctions. Merchants' Coffee-House, a coffeehouse located at the end of Wall Street in New York during the colonial era, hosted several auctions.[78] "The Merchants' [Coffee-House] was the location for frequent vendues of merchandise and commodities, ships and their cargoes, real estate and horses, as well as slaves."[79] When the American Revolution ended, Cornelius Bradford, the proprietor of Merchants' Coffee-House, sought to revitalize the (then) crippled American economy by strengthening the "coffeehouse." One of Bradford's preferred techniques for accomplishing this task was to restructure the distribution of market intelligence to coffeehouse patrons.[80] This included keeping records of ships arriving in port and recording the ships' origins and cargoes. This information would appear in newspapers under the title of *Bradford's Marine List* (similar in concept to that of Lloyd's *Marine List*).[81] "Bradford further established a register of merchants, a precursor to the first city directory of New York businesses."[82]

The actions taken by Bradford resulted in Merchants' Coffee-House "regain[ing] its following among the commercial elite of New York."[83] Soon afterward, a meeting would be held in Merchants' Coffee-House "to discuss proposals for a bank to provide credit for the fledgling republic, modelled on the Bank of England."[84] The merchants created the Bank of New York during this particular meeting to fulfill this role. The Bank of New York started out with $500,000 worth of capital, which was comprised of holdings of silver and gold.[85] Since the Bank of New York had proven to be a success, the same merchants held another meeting at Merchants' Coffee-House to reinstitute the Chamber of Commerce, initially established under British rule.[86] The role that coffeehouses played in the business practices of the new American Republic diversified soon after that as the emerging market for American stocks drew more attention.

The securities market that emerged in America during this time resembled its British counterpart.[87] "[S]tock transactions were concluded by brokers, acting as middlemen between specific customers, or by stockjobbers, who bought and sold for themselves."[88] Traders congregated on a regular basis for stock auctions. Stock auctions took place in the Long Room at the Merchants' Coffee-House, usually in the afternoon or evening.[89] "In the early 1790s the trade in bank stock in New York had begun to get out of control, exacerbated by the launch of rival subscriptions for a bizarre range of new banks and companies."[90] By 1792, many merchants and businesses had been ruined. In May of the same year, twenty-two stockbrokers held a meeting to discuss ways to develop a more sound structure for the stock market. These brokers subsequently decided to relocate to the upstairs room of Tontine Coffee-House, which was located on Wall Street.[91] A wide range of business activities took place in the Tontine Coffee-House. Everything from auctions, stock trading, and the organization of various insurance ventures occurred at one point or another within the coffeehouse.[92] "In 1796 [the Tontine Coffee-House] became the headquarters of a tontine of moneyed investors trading under the name of the New York Insurance Company."[93] The New York Insurance Company preceded the New York Stock and Exchange Board (NYSEB), which was established in 1817.[94] The NYSEB assumed a different name in 1863. The NYSEB (under a new name) would relocate several times to various transient locations within the vicinity of Wall Street. However, the volume of stock trades in which the organization engaged increased so sharply toward the end of the 19th century that they needed a larger and more tangible location more than ever. The NYSEB (under a different name) eventually relocated to a newly constructed headquarters in 1903. The trading floor in the newly constructed headquarters was one of the largest volumes of space in New York City at the time.

The financial markets that emerged from the coffee-houses of 18th century London and New York still have a commanding presence in today's society. New Lloyd's Coffee-House is known today as Lloyd's of London, the world's largest insurance market. The *Marine List* that was posted in Lloyd's Coffee-House, and later New Lloyd's, is today known as *Lloyd's List*. The stock exchange that emerged from New Jonathan's Coffee-House is now known as the London Stock Exchange. The NYSEB, whose origins lie in the Tontine Coffee-House, is now known as the New York Stock Exchange.

Analysis
From Jonathan's Coffee-House to the London Stock Exchange

Traders near the Royal Exchange would go to Jonathan's Coffee-House in order to conduct trading. It is important to point out, though, that the primary function of this venue was to serve coffee. When the majority of traders began to patronize Jonathan's Coffee-House for the purpose of trading and not to consume coffee, then the traders were being supplied with the services of a coffeehouse that they did not demand. Another way to look at this is that the traders in Jonathan's Coffee-House were being supplied with a trading environment that they were not demanding. The environment within the coffeehouse did not meet the needs of the stockbrokers who met there. Jonathan's Coffee-House was open to the public, and the stockbrokers who conducted their business there preferred to do business in private. This leaves one pondering why the stockbrokers of Jonathan's Coffee-House could not demand the services of a coffeehouse or a particular trading environment solely on the basis that they were being supplied to them. Well, based on the principal theory outlined in this book, the stockbrokers of Jonathan's Coffee-House had no incentive to demand the services of a coffeehouse simply because they were being supplied to them. They also did not have an incentive to demand a trading environment simply because it was being supplied to them.

Therefore:

(5a) $$SCH/TE \neq DCH/TE$$

Where:

SCH/TE = the act of supplying the stockbrokers of Jonathan's Coffee-House with the services of a coffeehouse / the act of supplying the stockbrokers of Jonathan's Coffee-House with an environment to conduct trading in

DCH/TE = the act of the stockbrokers of Jonathan's Coffee-House demanding the services of a coffeehouse / the act of the stockbrokers of Jonathan's Coffee-House demanding the trading environment within the coffeehouse

Supplying the stockbrokers of Jonathan's Coffee-House with the services of a coffeehouse did not result in the stockbrokers demanding the services of a coffeehouse because no incentive existed for them to demand these services just because they were being supplied. The same is true when considering why the stockbrokers of Jonathan's Coffee-House did not demand the trading environment that was being supplied to them. Now, as far as the services of a coffeehouse go, stockbrokers in Jonathan's Coffee-House did purchase coffee. However, that was not their primary reason for being there. The stockbrokers' demand for the ability to conduct their trading within Jonathan's Coffee-House far outweighed their demand for the services of a coffeehouse.

Therefore:

(5b)   DT > DCH

Where:

DT = the demand among the stockbrokers of Jonathan's Coffee-House for the ability to conduct their trading within Jonathan's Coffee-House

DCH = the demand among the stockbrokers of Jonathan's Coffee-House for the services of a coffeehouse

The stockbrokers of Jonathan's Coffee-House preferred trading stocks to drinking coffee. What the stockbrokers did not prefer, however, was the environment within the coffeehouse in which they traded. The fact that the stockbrokers of Jonathan's Coffee-House were being supplied with both the services of a coffeehouse and a trading environment, neither of which they demanded, generated a demand for the founding of a separate establishment in which they could conduct their trading.

Therefore:

(5c) $$(SCH/TE \neq DCH/TE) = DSE$$

Where:

$(SCH/TE \neq DCH/TE)$ = the disproportionate demand for the services of a coffeehouse among the stockbrokers of Jonathan's Coffee-House / the disproportionate demand among the stockbrokers of Jonathan's Coffee-House for the trading environment there

DSE = the demand for the establishment of a separate trading venue outside of Jonathan's Coffee-House / the demand for the establishment of the Stock Exchange, predecessor to the London Stock Exchange

Note: DSE represents a new form of a previously existing Demand. The stockbrokers of Jonathan's Coffee-House had always demanded a convenient location in which to trade. The stockbrokers' demand for a convenient trading location simply changed forms from a demand for the use of Jonathan's Coffee-House as a trading venue to a demand for the establishment of a separate trading venue (see The Law of Demand Conservation).

The demand for the establishment of a separate trading venue outside of Jonathan's Coffee-House resulted in the establishment (supplying) of a separate trading venue.

Therefore:

(5d) $$DSE = SSE$$

Where:

DSE = the demand for the establishment of a separate trading venue outside of Jonathan's Coffee-House

SSE = the establishment (supplying) of a separate trading venue outside of Jonathan's Coffee-House / the establishment of the Stock Exchange, predecessor to the London Stock Exchange

The act of supplying the stockbrokers of Jonathan's Coffee-House with the services of a coffeehouse did not cause the stockbrokers to demand the services of a coffeehouse. The stockbrokers of Jonathan's Coffee-House did not demand the poor trading environment that they were being supplied with either. However, the demand for a trading venue to be established outside of Jonathan's Coffee-House resulted in the Stock Exchange being established, which later became the London Stock Exchange. One of the underlying reasons was that there was no incentive for the stockbrokers of Jonathan's Coffee-House to demand the services of a coffeehouse or the trading environment there just because it was being supplied to them. There was an incentive, however, to supply the stockbrokers of Jonathan's Coffee-House with a separate venue in which they could conduct their trading just because they demanded one.

From Lloyd's Coffee-House to Lloyd's of London

Merchants frequented Lloyd's Coffee-House for the purpose of participating in auctions and to acquire intelligence pertaining to the shipping industry. Edward Lloyd exploited the shipping information that patrons exchanged in his coffeehouse and used it to establish his *Marine List*. After which, Lloyd's Coffee-House moved away from the practice of auctions and began to attract underwriters and intermediaries who were focused solely on the shipping industry. This resulted in Lloyd's Coffee-House becoming the center of the marine insurance business. The fact remains that at that point, Edward Lloyd was still running a coffeehouse whose primary function was to sell coffee, not marine insurance policies. When the majority of underwriters and intermediaries began to frequent Lloyd's Coffee-House due to its role in the marine insurance business, and not for its coffee, then that meant that the underwriters and intermediaries were being supplied with the services of a coffeehouse that they did not demand. The underwriters and intermediaries also became dissatisfied with the negligent business practices of the proprietor of Lloyd's Coffee-House. Thus, the underwriters and intermediaries of Lloyd's Coffee-House were also being supplied with a proprietorship that they were not demanding. The underwriters and intermediaries who occupied Lloyd's Coffee-House had no incentive to demand the services of a coffeehouse just because they were being supplied to them. They also had no incentive to demand the proprietorship of Lloyd's Coffee-House just because it was being supplied to them.

Therefore:

(6a) $SCH/P \neq DCH/P$

Where:
SCH/P = the act of supplying the underwriters and intermediaries of Lloyd's Coffee-House with the services of a coffeehouse / the act of supplying the underwriters and intermediaries of Lloyd's Coffee-House with a proprietorship

DCH/P = the act of the underwriters and intermediaries of Lloyd's Coffee-House demanding the services of a coffeehouse / the act of the underwriters and intermediaries of Lloyd's Coffee-House demanding the coffeehouse's proprietorship

Supplying the underwriters and intermediaries of Lloyd's Coffee-House with the services of a coffeehouse did not cause them to demand the services of a coffeehouse because no incentive existed for the underwriters and intermediaries to demand the services of a coffeehouse just because those services were being supplied to them. The underwriters and intermediaries also had no incentive to demand the proprietorship of Lloyd's Coffee-House simply because it was being supplied to them. The underwriters and intermediaries in Lloyd's Coffee-House did, in fact, purchase coffee. However, their demand for coffee was not proportionate to the supply. The underwriters' and intermediaries' *Demand* for the opportunity to conduct their business within Lloyd's Coffee-House superceded their *Demand* for coffee.

Therefore:

(6b) $DT > DCH$

Where:
DT = the demand among the underwriters and intermediaries in Lloyd's Coffee-House for the ability to conduct their business within the coffeehouse
DCH = the demand among the underwriters and intermediaries in Lloyd's Coffee-House for the services of a coffeehouse

It has been illustrated that the choice activity of the underwriters and intermediaries while in Lloyd's Coffee-House was to conduct business related to the marine insurance business, and not to consume coffee. Therefore, the underwriters and intermediaries were being supplied with the services of a coffeehouse that they did not demand. Also, the underwriters and intermediaries in Lloyd's Coffee-House were still being supplied with a proprietorship that they were not demanding. This resulted in a subsequent demand being generated for the establishment of a new headquarters for the marine insurance business.

Therefore:

(6c) $(SCH/P \neq DCH/P) = DNL$

Where:

$(SCH/P \neq DCH/P)$ = the disproportionate demand for the services of a coffeehouse among the underwriters and intermediaries who occupied Lloyd's Coffee-House / the disproportionate demand among the underwriters and intermediaries who occupied Lloyd's Coffee-House for the proprietorship being supplied to them

DNL = the demand for the establishment of a new headquarters for the marine insurance business among the underwriters and intermediaries who occupied Lloyd's Coffee-House

Note: DNL represents a new form of a previously existing Demand. The underwriters and intermediaries of the marine insurance business always demanded a suitable headquarters in which to conduct their business. The demand among the underwriters and intermediaries for a suitable headquarters for the marine insurance business simply changed forms from a demand to use Lloyd's Coffee-House as a headquarters to a demand for the establishment of a new headquarters (see The Law of Demand Conservation).

The demand among the underwriters and intermediaries of Lloyd's Coffee-House for the establishment of a new headquarters for the marine insurance business resulted in the establishment (supplying) of a new headquarters for the marine insurance business, New Lloyd's Coffee-House.

Therefore:

(6d) $DNL = SNL$

Where:
DNL = the demand for the establishment of a new headquarters for the marine insurance business among the underwriters and intermediaries who occupied Lloyd's Coffee-House
SNL = the establishment (supplying) of a new headquarters for the marine insurance business / the establishment of New Lloyd's Coffee-House, predecessor to Lloyd's of London

The underwriters and intermediaries who occupied Lloyd's Coffee-House were being supplied with both the services of a coffeehouse and the proprietorship of the coffeehouse. However, the underwriters and intermediaries demanded neither of these. One of the reasons for this (if not the primary or only reason) is that no incentive existed for the underwriters and intermediaries to demand either the services of the coffeehouse or the proprietorship of the coffeehouse just because it was being supplied to them. The underwriters and intermediaries subsequently demanded the establishment of a separate venue. In this particular case, a new venue was established, New Lloyd's Coffee-House. The reason New Lloyd's Coffee-House was established was because an incentive existed for it to be established (supplied) because of what the underwriters and intermediaries of Lloyd's Coffee-House were demanding.

From the Tontine Coffee-House to the New York Stock Exchange

The brokers who frequented the Tontine Coffee-House conducted their business in the coffeehouse's upstairs room. The behavior of the brokers in the Tontine Coffee-House may appear to be slightly different from their counterparts in Lloyd's and Jonathan's coffeehouses because they immediately sought the seclusion of an upstairs room rather than conducting their business on the coffeehouse's main floor. At any rate, the ambitions of the businessmen who occupied all three coffee-houses were aligned because they all made efforts to build organizations in which they could conduct business on a much grander scale than had previously been possible from within the coffeehouse. The sequence of events that led to the evolution of the business within the Tontine Coffee-House was reversed when compared to the events that led to the establishment of New Jonathan's and New Lloyd's coffeehouses. The New York Insurance Company, which began inside of the Tontine Coffee-House, reemerged as the New York Stock and Exchange Board (NYSEB)[95] before relocating to another venue. Without focusing on relocation at this point, one should consider how the New York Stock Exchange was created from an organization that originated in a coffeehouse and why the New York Stock Exchange is not in that very coffeehouse today. The reason is that the volume of trading done by the NYSEB increased so sharply that the upstairs room of the Tontine Coffee-House could no longer contain it. Thus, the Tontine Coffee-House was supplying the brokers of the NYSEB with a business environment that they did not demand. The actions taken by the Tontine Coffee-House to supply the brokers of the NYSEB with a particular business environment did not result in a demand for it by the brokers.

Therefore:

(7a)   SBE ≠ DBE

Where:
SBE = the act of the Tontine Coffee-House supplying the brokers of the NYSEB with a business environment
DBE = the act of the brokers of the NYSEB demanding the business environment being supplied to them by the Tontine Coffee-House

One discrepancy with the Tontine Coffee-House in respect to the other coffeehouses that hosted businessmen is that the brokers who occupied the Tontine Coffee-House went straight for the upstairs room when staking a claim to a place to conduct business. Thus, one should not consider the brokers' demand for the services of a coffeehouse in this particular application. What one must ultimately consider, however, is that the Tontine Coffee-House supplied the brokers of the NYSEB with a business environment that they did not demand. This resulted in generating a subsequent demand for relocation of their organization.

Therefore:

(7b)   (SBE ≠ DBE) = DLV

Where:

(SBE ≠ DBE) = disproportionate demand among the brokers of the NYSEB in respect to the business environment being supplied to them by the Tontine Coffee-House

DLV = demand among the brokers of the NYSEB to relocate their organization to a larger venue

Note: DLV represents a new form of a previously existing Demand. The brokers of the NYSEB had always demanded the use of a venue in which to conduct their trading. The demand among the brokers for the use of a specific trading venue changed forms from a demand for the use of the upstairs room of the Tontine Coffee-House as a trading venue to a demand for a larger trading venue (see The Law of Demand Conservation).

Because the brokers of the NYSEB demanded relocation to a larger venue, their demands were met.

Therefore:

(7c)   DLV = SLV

Where:

DLV = the act of the brokers of the NYSEB demanding relocation of their organization to a larger venue

SLV = the act of the brokers of the NYSEB supplying themselves with a larger venue / relocation of the NYSEB to a larger venue

The Tontine Coffee-House was supplying the brokers of the NYSEB with a particular business environment.

While we could deduce, because of the lack of room for trading, that the brokers of the NYSEB did not demand the business environment that the Tontine Coffee-House supplied to them, they also did not demand such a business environment because they had no incentive to demand it simply because it was being supplied to them. Subsequent demand for relocation to another venue in search of a better business environment resulted in relocation occurring, or the necessary means or actions necessary for it to occur being supplied to the brokers. Relocation of the NYSEB allowed it to evolve into the New York Stock Exchange of today.

Note: Relocation of the NYSEB occurred several times after the organization left the Tontine Coffee-House. One must assume that, in respect to this analysis, the application of the SDP Theorem to the first relocation is consistent with subsequent relocations.

D. *Irrational Goods*

A. The Fountain of Youth

The Fountain of Youth is a spring that reputedly restores youth to anyone who drinks its water. Legend has it that the Fountain of Youth's location is in Florida. This legend emerged from historical accounts of the efforts made by one Juan Ponce de León in the 16th century. Juan Ponce de León was a Spanish explorer who arrived in America on Columbus' second voyage in 1493. He became governor of Puerto Rico in 1509. It was while Ponce de León was governor of Puerto Rico that he first learned of the Fountain of Youth from its people. In 1513, Ponce de León led an expedition to the north in search of the Fountain of Youth. It was during this expedition that Ponce de León discovered Florida. However, he did not locate the Fountain of Youth during his expedition. Despite the fact that Ponce de León never found the Fountain of Youth, its legend and "demand" for it remains intact today.

When speaking of the "demand" for the Fountain of Youth, one must address specifically why people desire it. Every human being on the planet wants to reverse the aging process. This is the reason that Ponce de León made such an extraordinary effort to locate the Fountain of Youth and it is the reason that generations after him have sought it out. Therefore, we can say that there has been a collective demand for the Fountain of Youth throughout history. However, despite the "demand" for the Fountain of Youth, nobody has located it; thus nobody has supplied it.

Therefore:

(8a) $DFoY \neq SFoY$

Where:

DFoY = the act of society demanding the Fountain of Youth

SFoY = the act of the Fountain of Youth being discovered / the act of the Fountain of Youth being supplied

After examining the *Demand Side* of the SDP Model in 8a, it is evident that applying the SDP Model to the demand for irrational goods is rather complex. The average person who feels the effects of aging demands the ability to drink from the rejuvenating waters of the Fountain of Youth. Yet, the Fountain of Youth has never been supplied...or has it? In order to determine if someone has actually supplied the Fountain of Youth, one must consider what effects the Fountain of Youth is expected to have on an aging person. The Fountain of Youth is reputed to restore youth to anyone who drinks its water. But what is a clear definition of "youth restoration"? Does restoration of a youthful appearance qualify? What about "feeling" younger? In the modern era, medical advancements in cosmetic surgery and the establishment of venues such as relaxation spas support "youth restoration" efforts. Thus, an artificial Fountain of Youth exists today in various segments.

Therefore:

(8b) $DFoY = SAFoY$

Where:

DFoY = the act of society demanding the Fountain of Youth

SAFoY = the creating, and supplying, of an Artificial Fountain of Youth

The demand for the Fountain of Youth has resulted in advancements in modern-day society that may not have otherwise existed. For example, the medical profession has had a strong incentive to make advancements in plastic surgery techniques such as face-lifts and to develop drugs such as botulinum toxin (Botox) because of the demand for the Fountain of Youth or because of the fundamental demand among aging human beings to gain the ability to look and feel younger. However, society has had no incentive to demand advancements in cosmetic surgery simply because physicians and others have supplied them.

Therefore:

(8c) $SAFoY \neq DAFoY$

Where:

SAFoY = the act of an Artificial Fountain of Youth being supplied by various producers

DAFoY = the act of society demanding an Artificial Fountain of Youth

Note: Demand for the Fountain of Youth has remained intact for centuries and, thus, justifies the Law of Demand Conservation. Time has not destroyed the demand for the Fountain of Youth.

B. The History of Humans in Flight

The ability to fly is something that has intrigued humanity since the beginning of time. We can trace the earliest influences of human-developed flight to China around 400 B.C. It was around this time that the Chinese first developed kites. The Chinese had many uses for their kites. Among their uses for kites were religious ceremonies, weather condition tests, and recreation. Flying these kites led the Chinese to ponder whether it was possible for humans to fly. These kites marked a significant period in the history of flight, as they were the predecessor to both the balloon and the glider.[96] The centuries following the development of the Chinese kite represent numerous failures in people's attempts at flight. Among the most interesting attempts at flight were those that involved men strapping lightweight boards or wings made of feathers to their arms and attempting to fly. These attempts usually resulted in death. Despite the numerous failures in people's attempts to fly, society was determined to achieve flight. The Wright brothers were the first humans to achieve flight. Their first flight took place in 1903. It is important to note that between 400 B.C. and 1902 A.D., humankind demanded the ability to fly. However, nobody achieved flight during this period. Demanding the ability to fly did not result in it materializing in a timely manner.

Therefore:

(9a) $DF(1) \neq SF(1)$

Where:
$DF(1)$ = the act of humankind demanding the ability to fly
$SF(1)$ = the act of humankind supplying itself with the ability to fly

The disequilibrium displayed in the *Demand Side* of the SDP Model (see 9a) applies only to the period between 400 B.C. and 1902 A.D. The fact that people eventually gained the ability to fly justifies the *Demand Side* of the SDP Model in this specific scenario.

Therefore:

(9b) $$DF(1) = SF(2)$$

Where:
$DF(1)$ = the act of humankind demanding the ability to fly
$SF(2)$ = the act of humankind eventually supplying itself with the ability to fly

An incentive existed for the Wright brothers to supply the ability for people to fly simply because society demanded it.

Note: Demand for humankind to achieve flight remained intact for roughly twenty-four centuries and, thus, was never destroyed (see The Law of Demand Conservation).

C. Beyond the Stars

The space race heated up (ironically) during the Cold War. It officially began when the former Union of Soviet Socialist Republics (U.S.S.R.) launched the world's first human-made satellite, Sputnik 1, on October 4, 1957. The space race climaxed when NASA's Apollo Program success-fully landed a manned mission (Apollo 11) on the moon on July 20, 1969. Further significant advances in space explora-tion include events such as the launch of the Hubble Space

Telescope in 1990 and the launch of the Mars Pathfinder in 1996. Society's interest in the stars did not begin, however, with the space race. Modern astronomy originated in ancient Greece. The Ancient Greeks made observations of the sky and developed sound explanations based on what they saw. In his writings, Aristotle summarized the ancient Greeks' knowledge of the stars. Aristotle was able to attribute the moon's transforming shape to the various ways the sun illuminates the moon's surface over the course of one month. He was also able to determine that the sun is farther away from the earth than the moon because the moon passes in front of the sun during a solar eclipse.[97] Aristotle probably would have enjoyed walking on the moon's surface or examining the stars in greater detail. The items that would have allowed him to do so, such as Apollo 11 and the Hubble Space Telescope, were far from his reach. In short, the ability to conduct advanced space exploration was not at the disposal of the ancient world. *Advanced Space Exploration* is a collective designation of modern advances in space exploration and appears illustrated below.

Advanced Space Exploration = [Sputnik 1 + Apollo 11 + Hubble Space Telescope + Mars Pathfinder]

Even though there is no evidence that astronomers of the ancient world made specific demands for satellites or rockets, their efforts to further explore the stars indicates that they demanded the ability to access the information that could be collected only with the use of such items. However, the demand among astronomers of the ancient world for *Advanced Space Exploration* did not result in someone supplying it to them.

Therefore:

(10a) $DASE(1) \neq SASE(1)$

Where:

$DASE(1)$ = the act of the astronomers of the ancient world demanding *Advanced Space Exploration*

$SASE(1)$ = the act of the ancient world supplying itself with *Advanced Space Exploration*

While the demand among the astronomers of the ancient world for *Advanced Space Exploration* did not result in it being supplied to them specifically, their demand resulted in the ability to conduct *Advanced Space Exploration* being supplied to future generations.

Therefore:

(10b) $DASE(1) = SASE(2)$

Where:

$DASE(1)$ = the act of the astronomers of the ancient world demanding *Advanced Space Exploration*

$SASE(2)$ = the act of the modern world supplying itself with *Advanced Space Exploration*

The demand for *Advanced Space Exploration* has remained intact for centuries and, thus, has never been destroyed (see *The Law of Demand Conservation*). The modern world has not demanded *Advanced Space Exploration* specifically because it has been supplied to them. The modern world has demanded *Advanced Space Exploration* because it retained the demand that was passed down from the ancient world and, subsequently, demanded it themselves.

E. Illegal Markets

A. The Market for Contract Killers

Contract killing has existed in one form or another throughout history. Contract killing usually occurs as a scenario in which two parties enter into an agreement where one person agrees to kill a pre-identified person or persons on behalf of another person in exchange for some form of compensation (typically money). Throughout history, people have hired contract killers for reasons that vary greatly. Many people can relate to the typical scenario of someone, such as a mob boss, ordering somebody to be "whacked." The Mafia typically makes use of contract killers in order to secure an alibi. That way the individuals who want somebody dead can make sure they are in a public setting where many people can attest to their whereabouts when the murder is to take place, thus, prematurely removing themselves from a list of primary suspects. The fact remains that contract killers have existed throughout time simply because people have demanded their services. Contract killers have always had an incentive to supply their services because there has always been a demand for them.

Therefore:

(11a)   DCK = SCK

Where:
DCK = the act of the general public demanding the services of contract killers

SCK = the act of contract killers supplying the general public with their services

Note: Hiring a contract killer is illegal in virtually every jurisdiction. Despite this fact, people continue to demand the services of contract killers. Thus, declaring the act of hiring a contract killer as an illegal act has not caused the demand for contract killers to be destroyed (see The Law of Demand Conservation).

No individual has ever had an incentive to demand the services of a contract killer just because someone was providing those services.

Therefore:

(11b) $SCK \neq DCK$

Where:
SCK = the act of contract killers supplying the general public with their services
DCK = the act of the general public demanding the services of contract killers

There have also been past incidents where various law enforcement officials have "moonlighted" as contract killers for the mob. The Mafia has always demanded the services of contract killers. The fact that they have used law enforcement officials as contract killers means that they were demanding more than just ordinary assassins. They were demanding contract killers who were required to maintain firearms proficiency, which taxpayers paid for. They were also demanding contract killers who could easily evade law enforcement officials due to their own law enforcement credentials. Therefore, it would be safe to say that law enforcement officials employed by the Mafia as assassins are "Trojan horses." Law enforcement officials who have supplied their services as contract killers to the mob have transcended legal barriers in the process due to the incentive they would receive for doing so. The fact that legal barriers have been broken in this particular scenario illustrates just how strong the market forces are in relation to the *Demand Side* of the SDP Model. The underlying principle here is that the Mafia did not have an incentive to demand the services of Trojan horses simply because law enforcement officials supplied them. Trojan horses, on the other hand, had an incentive to supply their services as contract killers simply because the Mafia demanded their services.

Therefore:

(11c)   DTH = STH

Where:
DTH = the act of the Mafia demanding the services of Trojan Horses
STH = the act of Trojan Horses supplying the Mafia with the services of a contract killer

B. The International Drug Trade

The international drug trade generates billions of dollars in revenue each year. One question that people always raise in relation to the international drug trade is how does an industry, which is illegal and combated by every law enforcement organization on the planet, manage to maintain its existence as well as generate superior profits? The answer is *Demand*. Global demand for illegal drugs is so high that drug cartels go to extraordinary lengths to supply their products. Producers of illegal drugs willfully break the law and risk competitors murdering them just to sell drugs. Also, narco-terrorists (or terrorists working under contract for drug cartels) have been known to carry out assassinations and other terrorist-related activities just to ensure that their employers can successfully supply their product. Such actions indicate the existence of a strong incentive for drug cartels to supply their products. The fact is that drug cartels and other independent drug dealers supply illegal drugs simply because they are being demanded, nothing more.

Therefore:

(12a) $DID = SID$

Where:
DID = the act of society demanding illegal drugs
SID = the act of drug cartels / independent drug dealers supplying illegal drugs

Drug dealers may very well supply illegal drugs simply because people demand them. However, no scenario exists, neither past nor present, where a consumer of illegal drugs demands them just because drug dealers supply them.

Therefore:

(12b) $SID \neq DID$

Where:

SID = the act of drug cartels / independent drug dealers supplying illegal drugs

DID = the act of society demanding illegal drugs

It is of interest to note that the *Demand Side* relationship displayed in 12a provides such a strong incentive to the suppliers of illegal drugs that illegal drugs find their way into places that one would least expect. A maximum-security penitentiary is such a place. It is hard to believe that prisoners locked behind concrete walls and steel bars would have the ability to access illegal substances. The fact that these prisoners demand illegal drugs causes suppliers to emerge in order to meet their demand. But prisoners are not in a position to pay for substances such as marijuana or cocaine. This is why it is important to consider the *Law of Demand Conservation* in this scenario. The prisoners' demand for illegal drugs is so tenacious that it cannot be destroyed, but can easily be transferred to individuals on the outside, such as family members. Family members or friends can then purchase drugs on behalf of their incarcerated loved ones and smuggle them into the penitentiary during visitation periods. If guards regularly search family members during these visitation periods, then family members can share an incentive (bribe) with a corrections officer, thus allowing the continued flow of illegal drugs into penitentiaries.

Society, in no way, shape, or form, demands illegal drugs simply because someone is supplying drugs to them. The only reason the international drug trade emerged and continues to remain in existence to this day, despite the efforts of various law enforcement organizations, is because drug cartels and drug dealers have an incentive to supply their products simply because their products are being demanded. Thus, the buyers of illegal drugs, not the suppliers of them, drive the international drug trade. Therefore, the aggressive efforts of law enforcement organizations to go after the suppliers of illegal drugs are inefficient since the consumers of such products are the only reason the drug cartels exist. And, in respect to the *Law of Demand Conservation*, the demand for illegal drugs can never be destroyed. Therefore, punishing consumers of such substances is equally as pointless.

C. Distribution of Alcoholic Beverages During the Prohibition Era

The Market for Laws dealt specifically with the market for the laws prohibiting the manufacture, sale, or transportation of alcohol within the United States. However, one should not just consider the market for the laws that prohibited alcohol when considering the SDP Theorem. One should also consider the market for alcohol itself during the Prohibition era. Ironically, the market for alcohol remained intact during the Prohibition era. Average Americans who wanted to consume alcohol during the thirteen years that Prohibition was in effect could if they chose to. Even though alcohol was illegal during Prohibition, people still demanded it. The fact that people were demanding alcohol during the Prohibition era provided an incentive for producers of alcoholic beverages to transcend legal barriers in order to supply alcohol.

Therefore:

(13a)   DAlcoholic Beverages = SAlcoholic Beverages

Where:

DAlcoholic Beverages = the act of Americans demanding alcoholic beverages during the Prohibition era

SAlcoholic Beverages = the act of producers of alcoholic beverages illegally producing and supplying them to Americans during the Prohibition era

Note: Despite the emplacement of legal barriers that prohibited anyone from purchasing alcohol (such as the 18th Amendment to the U.S. Constitution), Americans' demand for alcohol was never destroyed during the Prohibition era (see The Law of Demand Conservation).

It is important to note at this point, however, that even though Americans clearly demanded alcoholic beverages during the Prohibition era, they did not demand them simply because someone supplied them.

Therefore:

(13b)   SAlcoholic Beverages ≠ DAlcoholic Beverages

Where:

SAlcoholic Beverages = the act of producers of alcoholic beverages illegally producing and supplying them to Americans during the Prohibition era

DAlcoholic Beverages = the act of Americans demanding alcoholic beverages during the Prohibition era

The *Demand Side* relationship displayed in 13a provided such a strong incentive to producers of alcohol that gangsters, like the infamous Al Capone, resorted to the use of mob violence in order to take control of the market for illegal alcohol. Most people are familiar with the intimidation tactics used by gangsters during the Prohibition era in order to strengthen their position in the market for supplying alcoholic beverages. A scenario that better illustrates this concept is that of a mob boss ensuring steady demand for the product. For example, let's say that a few "associates" of a mob boss approach the owner of a speakeasy and ask the owner to purchase their "product." If the owner refuses, he or she will be "dealt with violently." Thus, the owner of the speakeasy has a choice: continue buying the mob's booze or die. Some may see this concept as a contradiction of the *Law of Demand Conservation* because organized crime syndicates of the Prohibition era apparently found a way to "create" demand for their product. On the contrary, they did not create demand for their product. When gangsters threatened speakeasy owners with death, they always demanded the ability to live. They bought alcohol from the mob because they wanted to continue to live. Giving the speakeasy owners a choice between buying alcohol from the mob or dying resulted in their demand for the ability to live changing forms and becoming a demand for the mob's alcohol.

F. Labor Markets

Labor markets are very interesting because they involve the least tangible of goods. Labor is not a good that can be sold on store shelves, which makes application of the SDP Theorem to labor markets quite interesting. Each and every employee of each and every organization in the world is a supplier of labor. They work for their employers and, thus, supply them with labor. The employers, being the consumers of such labor, are responsible for demanding it. Employers are not likely, however, to demand labor from their employees simply because their employees are supplying it to them.

Therefore:

(14a) $SL \neq DL$

Where:
SL = the act of employees supplying labor to their employers
DL = the act of employers demanding the labor being supplied to them by their employees

Supplying employers with labor will not result in employers demanding it because no incentive exists for employers to demand labor simply because it is being supplied to them. As an illustration, consider massive layoffs and unemployment in general. The fact that there have been many incidents where major corporations have laid off large portions of their labor force indicates that there is no incentive for employers to demand labor simply because workers are supplying it to them. If the opposite were true, employers would never lay off anyone. The same is true when considering the concept of unemployment. Unemployed workers, at least the ones who are actively seeking employment, are constantly attempting to supply their labor to employers. If employers were willing to demand this labor simply because unemployed workers were attempting to supply it to them then, theoretically, unemployment would not exist.[98]

Now that we have examined labor markets from the *Supply Side*, it is time to examine them from the *Demand Side*. The best examples that we can use to apply the *Demand Side* of the SDP Model to labor markets were addressed in the *Illegal Markets* section. The reason illegal labor provides a good example is because it once again illustrates how strong demand can be within a market. Markets are demand driven if individuals are willing to break the law in order to supply illegal labor simply because someone is demanding it. The labor being supplied by the likes of contract killers and drug dealers has been, and currently is being, readily demanded. Individuals belonging to both of these professions have always had an incentive to supply their labor in a specific illegal capacity simply because consumers have demanded it.

Therefore:

(14b) $DL = SL$

Where:
DL = the act of an individual demanding labor
SL = the act of an individual supplying labor

Further analysis of labor markets in respect to the SDP Theorem allows one to revisit the concept of a Trojan horse, described previously when examining the *Market for Contract Killers*. Rather than considering the labor practices of law enforcement officials who earned extra cash as assassins, one should now consider individuals called "drug mules." Drug mules use their bodies as containers to smuggle drugs across international lines. They usually accomplish this by swallowing several latex containers filled with illegal substances such as cocaine or heroin. The "mule" then boards a plane or boat that is bound for another country. Upon arrival, the drug mules "pass" the latex containers, which a drug dealer then collects. The mule receives some form of monetary compensation for this feat. Drug mules supply their labor in the same manner that any other drug trafficker would. What makes the labor supplied by the mule so attractive is that it is harder to detect drugs inside a human on a plane than it is to detect drugs smuggled inside a steel drum on a boat. The drug mules are thus Trojan horses. They have an incentive to supply their labor as Trojan horses simply because the drug lords demand it.

Therefore:

(14c) $DL/TH = SL/TH$

Where:
DL/TH = the act of Drug Lords demanding labor provided by Drug Mules / Trojan Horses
SL/TH = the act of Drug Mules / Trojan Horses supplying Drug Lords with labor

Drug lords have never demanded the labor that drug mules supply to them simply because the drug mules have been supplying it. The reason is that no incentive exists for a drug lord to perform such an action. There is an incentive, however, for drug mules to supply their labor simply because drug lords demand it. It is also important to point out that the law is equally as harsh on the drug mules as it is on drug lords. Yet both drug lords and drug mules continue to flourish because of the strength of the SDP Model's *Demand Side*.

G. The Market for Pollution

One may have never considered the concept of a *Market for Pollution*. However, if one can consider some of the most fundamental concepts relating to market forces, then one can say that pollution is "supplied" worldwide on a daily basis. Any individual who drives a car, flies an airplane, or consumes energy created from the burning of fossil fuels contributes to the global supply of pollution. And, of course, there is no incentive for anyone to demand pollution simply because it is being supplied to them. Actually, there appears to be no incentive for a living being to demand pollution for any reason. Trees and other assorted vegetation appear to be the only exception. Trees, as well as ocean-based vegetation and organisms such as seaweed, algae, and plankton remove carbon dioxide (CO_2) from the atmosphere (carbon sequestration) and incorporate it into biomass through the process of photosynthesis. Photosynthesis is the process in which plants and other organisms absorb CO_2 from the atmosphere, store the CO_2 as sugars, starch, or cellulose, and subsequently release oxygen as a waste product. Various forms of vegetation and other organisms require CO_2 for their fundamental growth processes and, thus, demand pollution. However, there does remain some ambiguity regarding a *Demand Side* application in this particular scenario. No one has identified a tangible "supplier" of CO_2 nor has anyone elaborated on the role of incentives in this particular application. What one should know at this point is that various forms of vegetation and other organisms demand CO_2, while someone or something supplies it. This concept requires one to differentiate between the different types of CO_2 production. We can then attribute CO_2 production to two parties: humankind and nature. Some irony may be present in such a distinction since humans are technically part of nature and emit CO_2 into the atmosphere through a natural respiratory process. Despite such ironies, nature produces CO_2 by way of volcanic outgassing, combustion of organic matter, and by the respiration processes of living aerobic organisms. Volcanic outgassing involves the release of CO_2 from beneath the earth's surface via a volcano into the atmosphere. Production of CO_2 because of the combustion of organic matter is simply the production of CO_2 because of burning organic material. CO_2 production by way of the respiration processes of living aerobic organisms is a cyclic process in which air-breathing creatures (including humans) inhale oxygen while subsequently exhaling CO_2. Human-made production of CO_2 results from a variety of things such as factories, automobiles, energy plants, and so on. One should also be aware that vegetation demand for CO_2 existed long before the human-made production of CO_2 began. Nature has always had an incentive to supply vegetation and other organisms with CO_2 because the process of supplying them with CO_2 helps maintain a balance of greenhouse gases within the atmosphere, inversely related to the amount of plant life on the earth's surface. Thus, we have identified a "supplier" of CO_2 and a plausible role of incentives for the *Demand Side* application in this scenario.

Therefore:

(15a)   DCarbon Dioxide = SCarbon Dioxide

Where:

DCarbon Dioxide = the act of various forms of vegetation and other organisms demanding Carbon Dioxide

SCarbon Dioxide = the act of "nature" supplying Carbon Dioxide to various forms of vegetation and other organisms

Environmental activists have sought to exploit the strength of the *Demand Side* application displayed in 15a. Environmental initiatives such as the Kyoto Protocol have called for the use of carbon dioxide sinks in order to reduce the amount of CO_2 emitted into the atmosphere. Carbon dioxide sinks, simply put, are carbon reservoirs. The natural versions of these "sinks" include forests and oceans. We consider forests to be carbon reservoirs because they are comprised of a large number of trees, which absorb CO_2. We consider oceans to be carbon reservoirs because of the plant life and organisms present in them that are capable of absorbing CO_2 (i.e., seaweed and plankton). The trees, seaweed, and plankton that make up these carbon dioxide sinks all demand CO_2 and it is this *Demand* that the framers of the Kyoto Protocol have successfully taken advantage of.

Another aspect of the *Market for Pollution* deals with those groups of people who want to gain the ability to release more CO_2 into the atmosphere rather than reducing it. Industrial firms, for example, rely on the combustion of fossil fuels in order to fulfill their energy production requirements. The combustion of fossil fuels in these firms results in large quantities of CO_2 being released into the atmosphere. Environmental initiatives, such as the Kyoto Protocol, have placed mandates on large industrial firms to reduce the amount of CO_2 that they emit into the atmosphere. In order to accomplish this task, the government required that industrial firms reduce the amount of fossil fuels that they burned on a daily basis. This process subsequently reduced the amount of energy available to these firms on a daily basis, thus, significantly reducing their production capabilities. A reduction in production capabilities translated into a reduction in revenues for these firms. Subsequent to this, industrial firms found themselves in a dilemma. These firms needed to maintain enough energy production in order to maximize their production and, thus, maximize their profits. Apparently, transforming their production lines to rely on alternate sources of energy that are cleaner than fossil fuels would take too much time and incur too great a cost. So industrial firms were stuck with trying to find a way to continue burning fossil fuels at the levels they previously had been without breaching the conditions that several environmental initiatives mandated. Various emissions-trading programs emerged subsequent to the demand for industrial firms to maintain their ability to burn fossil fuels at their desired levels. Governmental organizations as well as the private sector have fostered these emissions-trading programs. The private sector emissions-trading programs are among the most lucrative, generating millions of dollars for asset managers who oversee the trading of emissions credits for large industrial firms. Under a standard emissions-trading program, each country operates under the parameters of an allotted amount of CO_2 emissions per a given period. For example, an industrial firm in the United States may want to increase its productivity. To do so, the firm would need to increase its energy consumption and, thus, increase its CO_2 emissions. Such an increase may breach the allotted amount of CO_2 emissions for that particular firm in that particular region of the world. Thus, the American firm may endeavor to purchase emissions credits from a firm in India. Purchasing these credits may mean that the Indian firm will have to reduce CO_2 emissions for two weeks out of each month for one year, while the American firm that purchased the credits gets to increase its CO_2 emissions for two weeks a month for one year. The Indian firm would no doubt have to decrease its productivity in order to reduce its CO_2 emissions. However, the genius of such a program allows for compensating the Indian firm for its reduction in productivity because of the revenue it received from selling its emissions credits to the American firm. Therefore, one firm gets to increase its productivity while another receives compensation for decreasing its productivity; all the while, the overall global emissions of CO_2 are unaffected. Thus, the demand among industrial firms to gain the ability to maintain energy consumption levels while staying within the parameters of various environmental protocols results in an emissions-trading system emerging.

Therefore:

(15b)   DMEC/ETP = SMEC/ETP

Where:

DMEC/ETP = the act of global industrial firms demanding the ability to maintain their desired levels of energy consumption / the act of global industrial firms demanding a standardized emissions-trading program

SMEC/ETP = the act of governmental organizations and asset managers supplying global industrial firms with the ability to maintain their desired levels of energy consumption / the act of governmental organizations and asset managers supplying global industrial firms with a standardized emissions-trading program

Many governments and asset managers in the developed world have had an incentive to supply their domestic industries with an emissions trading program just because these industries were demanding it. The incentive for the governments would be to maintain economic growth within their respective countries and the incentive for the asset managers would be to maintain their own economic growth. No incentive existed, however, for these industrial firms to demand various emissions trading programs simply because governments and asset managers were supplying them.

Therefore:

(15c) $SMEC/ETP \neq DMEC/ETP$

Where:
SMEC/ETP = the act of governmental organizations and asset managers supplying global industrial firms with the ability to maintain their desired levels of energy consumption / the act of governmental organizations and asset managers supplying global industrial firms with a standardized emissions-trading program
DMEC/ETP = the act of global industrial firms demanding the ability to maintain their desired levels of energy consumption / the act of global industrial firms demanding a standardized emissions-trading program

The *Market for Pollution* does, in fact, extend past CO_2 production. Solid waste and domestic garbage, which pile up on curbsides and landfills all across the world, are forms of pollution. No one, per se, demands garbage. People do, however, demand that their garbage be disposed of.

Therefore:

(15d)   DGD = SGD

Where:
DGD = the act of the average person demanding that his or her garbage be disposed of
SGD = the act of specific firms supplying the average person with garbage disposal services

Specific firms responsible for garbage disposal had an incentive to emerge in order to meet the demand of the average citizen. However, members of the general population did not, and still do not, have an incentive to demand the services of a firm specializing in garbage disposal simply because they are being supplied.

Therefore:

(15e)   SGDS ≠ DGDS

Where:
SGDS = the act of specialized firms supplying garbage disposal services
DGDS = the act of the general population demanding garbage disposal services

The *Demand Side* relationship illustrated in 15d provided such a strong incentive to suppliers of garbage disposal services that organizations, such as the Mafia, resorted to illegal tactics in order to retain control over the garbage disposal market. Once upon a time in New York City, the Mafia reigned over a garbage cartel. They used various illegal tactics in order to control a garbage collecting market that was worth over a billion dollars a year.

H. *Wanted: Dead or Alive*

Most people are familiar with the typical images of the "Wild West" that include posters nailed to the side of a building with the heading "Wanted: Dead or Alive." These posters would typically include a picture of the wanted individual and the amount of money offered for capturing him or her. In the Wild West, some local governing body or another organization that had a stake in capturing a particular individual would reward the money. But why would any government (county, state, or federal) offer a reward for the capture of an individual when they already pay their own trained professionals such as a sheriff or a U.S. marshal? The reason is that offering a reward for the capture of a specific criminal gives the average citizen an incentive to find the individual in question and increases the overall number of bodies engaged in the search for the specific criminal. The more bodies there are actively engaged in a search for a criminal, the easier it is to find that criminal. What is of interest when considering this specific scenario is the "incentive" the average citizen receives for capturing a "wanted" criminal. The governing bodies described in the above scenario demanded the capture of specific individuals, and by offering a bounty, gave average citizens an incentive to supply their services as "bounty hunters."

Therefore:

(16a)   DSBH = SSBH

Where:
DSBH = the act of a specific governing body demanding the capture of a specific person / the act of a specific governing body demanding the services of a Bounty Hunter
SSBH = the act of a citizen supplying his or her services as a Bounty Hunter

Bounty hunters have always had an incentive to supply their services just because they were being demanded. However, governing bodies, such as those in the Wild West have never had an incentive to demand the services of bounty hunters simply because the bounty hunters were supplying them.

Therefore:

(16b) $SSBH \neq DSBH$

Where:
SSBH = the act of a citizen supplying his or her services as a Bounty Hunter
DSBH = the act of a specific governing body demanding the services of a Bounty Hunter

Various governing bodies have exploited the strength of the *Demand Side* of the SDP Model (See 16a) for centuries in order to capture criminals, terrorists, and other high-value targets. One very distinct exception to this scenario would be the situation surrounding the hunt for Osama bin Laden. A $25 million bounty was levied on his head in the wake of the September 11th terrorist attacks. The bounty was later raised to $50 million. However, to this date, no one has turned him in. No matter where bin Laden has been, it is likely that a significant number of people have seen him and/or know of his whereabouts. Yet no one who has been close to bin Laden appears to have had a need to increase his or her income. Otherwise, someone would have turned him over to the federal government in return for a multimillion-dollar bounty. The reason that no one has yet turned in Osama bin Laden may be that the people who surround him are jihadists. Jihadists are soldiers of a jihad, which is an Islamic term for "holy war." The jihadists who belong to bin Laden's jihad receive a "holy" incentive for maintaining their loyalty to bin Laden.[99] Such loyalties are apparently worth more than $50 million. Also, the lives of the jihadists, as well as the lives of their families, may have been endangered had they revealed the location of bin Laden. Thus, the *Demand Side* relationship illustrated in 16a is valid only if the bounty offered is enough to compensate the bounty hunter for the severances of any loyalties or personal convictions.

I. The Art of Speculation

Speculation in financial markets involves the buying and holding of certain goods and valuable materials for the express purpose of profiting from fluctuations in the price of such goods. Speculation differs somewhat from other roles taken in financial markets such as hedging and arbitrage. The role of a speculator within a financial market fits in quite well with the concepts of the SDP Theorem. For example, a speculator may purchase bushels of wheat in the commodities market with the intention of selling the wheat for a profit. However, unlike stocks, the bushels of wheat will not generate any dividends for the speculator. Also, the speculator may be located on Wall Street and, therefore, not have any immediate functional use for wheat. Thus, there is no incentive for a speculator to engage in the wheat trade other than the potential of making a profit from the sale of the wheat. The profit that the speculator seeks to make depends solely on the strength of the *Demand Side* of the SDP Model. Consumers demand wheat and farmers have an incentive to supply it.

Therefore:

(17a) $$DW = SW$$

Where:
DW = the act of consumers demanding wheat
SW = the act of farmers / wheat suppliers supplying wheat

A speculator could exploit the *Demand Side* relationship displayed in 17a by assuming the role of a wheat supplier. By purchasing and holding bushels of wheat, the speculator places himself or herself in a position to allow the forces of *Demand* to increase his or her revenue. For example, if harsh weather conditions significantly affected wheat production in the United States, then there would be a sharp decrease in the wheat supply. A decrease in the supply of wheat accompanied by a corresponding demand, either maintaining its previous levels or increasing, would cause the price of wheat to increase. If the speculator had previously purchased one hundred bushels of wheat at the price of $20 a bushel and the decline in wheat production resulted in the price rising to $50 a bushel, then the speculator could make a $3,000 profit by selling his or her wheat. Thus, the speculator would have an incentive to supply wheat, something he or she had no immediate use for, simply because consumers were demanding it.

Therefore:

(17b)   DW = SW

Where:
DW = the act of consumers demanding wheat
SW = the act of speculators supplying wheat

However, consumers of wheat in such a scenario would not have an incentive to demand wheat simply because speculators were supplying it.

Therefore:

(17c) $SW \neq DW$

Where:
SW = the act of speculators supplying wheat
DW = the act of consumers demanding wheat

VI.

CONCLUSION

This book redefines the laws of supply and demand. Previous techniques used to analyze the factors of supply and demand have involved constructing graphs in order to determine what price a good or service could bring within a market. Unlike the graphs, the paradoxical relationship identified in this book between *Supply* and *Demand* allows one to examine the rational motivations of both producers and consumers. An incentive does not exist for consumers to demand a good or service simply because a producer supplies it, whereas an incentive does exist for a producer to supply a good or service simply because consumers demand it. Just as the saying goes, "You can lead a horse to water, but you can't make it drink." A person can supply a horse with water or the opportunity to drink water, but he or she cannot make it drink because no incentive exists for a horse to drink (or demand) water simply because someone is supplying it to the horse. Some may question the existence of several of the "markets" identified in this book. However, despite how one may typically view a traditional market, there is a basis for market analysis in any scenario where a good or service is being supplied, demanded, or both. This book has also provided some considerable insight into how we can use the function of markets to analyze a diverse array of topics such as political science, evolutionary biology, the origin of financial markets, and organized crime. Further investigation of the theory outlined in this book should allow one to explore additional applications of its theory as well. At this point, we should achieve the standardization of the notion that analysis of markets must not begin with both *Supply* and *Demand* but simply with *Demand*. This book proves that *Demand* is the stronger of the two. It doesn't matter what actions are taken by the state to curtail market activity. Whether it is a trade embargo, tariff, or the establishment of a pure command economy, the market will always go in the direction that consumers want, period. Markets, wherever they may be, are demand based. The *Demand* factor in such markets represents a significant degree of tenacity, because, as stated in the *Law of Demand Conservation, Demand* cannot be created or destroyed, but can only change from one form to another. Such a concept becomes evident when considering the notion that society's demand for things, such as the ability to fly and to further space exploration, have remained intact for centuries and, thus, have never been destroyed. Also, society's demand for goods such as the Fountain of Youth, has changed forms from a demand for the Fountain of Youth to a demand for an artificial version. Another point can be made regarding the notion that *Demand* for this book cannot be created. That is because demand for this book has actually existed for centuries (in a broader form) because society has always demanded new advances in economic theory. Producers must know that *Demand*, in various shapes and forms, may already exist for their goods and services prior to their being supplied. The *Demand* for goods or services cannot be created, but must be uncovered as if it were a buried treasure.

Notes

[1] The terms "good" and "service" are included in the SDP Theorem on a general basis and may be modified in relation to the specific application of the theorem.

[2] Thomas R. Pegram, *Battling Demon Rum: The Struggle for a Dry America, 1800-1933* (Chicago: Ivan R. Dee, 1998), 3.

[3] Ibid.

[4] Ibid.

[5] Ibid., 136.

[6] Ibid., 139.

[7] Ibid.

[8] Ibid., 136.

[9] "Constitution of the United States: Amendments 11-27," The U.S. National Archives and Records Administration, http://www.archives.gov/national-archives-experience/charters/constitution_amendments_11-27.html.

[10] Thomas R. Pegram, *Battling Demon Rum: The Struggle for a Dry America, 1800-1933* (Chicago: Ivan R. Dee, 1998), 158.

[11] Ibid., 176.

[12] Ibid., 159.

[13] Ibid.

[14] Ibid., 181.

[15] Ibid., 184-185.

[16] Ibid., 185.

[17] Ibid.

[18] Ibid.

[19] "Constitution of the United States: Amendments 11-27," The U.S. National Archives and Records Administration, http://www.archives.gov/national-archives-experience/charters/constitution_amendments_11-27.html.

[20] Data pertaining to an exact figure of Americans who did not abide by the 18th Amendment is hard to come by. What one should acknowledge at this point is that the majority of American politicians approved the 21st Amendment to the U.S. Constitution. Since, in theory, the motivations of these politicians collectively mirrored those of the American public, then we can assume that the majority of Americans were in favor of the 21st Amendment. We can also assume that those Americans who were in favor of the 21st Amendment were opposed to the 18th Amendment and, consequently, did not abide by it.

[21] Jennifer A. Clack, *Gaining Ground: The Origin and Evolution of Tetrapods* (Indiana: Indiana University Press, 2002), 1.

[22] Ibid., 1-2.

[23] Ibid., 15.

[24] Ibid., 16.

[25] Barrell, J. 1916. Influence of Silurian-Devonian climates on the rise of air-breathing vertebrates. *Bulletin of the Geological Society of America* 27: 387-436.

Lull, R.S. 1918. *The Pulse of Life: The Evolution of the Earth.* New Haven, Conn.: Yale University Press. Quoted in Jennifer A. Clack, *Gaining Ground: The Origin and Evolution of Tetrapods* (Indiana: Indiana University Press, 2002), 99.

[26] Jennifer A. Clack, *Gaining Ground: The Origin and Evolution of Tetrapods* (Indiana: Indiana University Press, 2002), 99.

[27] Ibid., 99-100.

[28] Romer, A.S. 1933. *Man and the Vertebrates.* Chicago: Chicago University Press.

Romer, A.S. 1945. *Vertebrate Paleontology.* 2nd edition. Chicago: Chicago University Press.

Romer, A.S. 1958. Tetrapod limbs and early tetrapod life. *Evolution* 12: 365-369.

Quoted in Jennifer A. Clack, *Gaining Ground: The Origin and Evolution of Tetrapods* (Indiana: Indiana University Press, 2002), 100.

[29] Orton, G.L. 1954. Original adaptive significance of the tetrapod limb. *Science* 120: 1042-1043. Quoted in Jennifer A. Clack, *Gaining Ground: The Origin and Evolution of Tetrapods* (Indiana: Indiana University Press, 2002), 100.

[30] Ewer, D.W. 1955. Tetrapod limb. *Science* 122: 467. Quoted in Jennifer A. Clack, *Gaining Ground: The Origin and Evolution of Tetrapods* (Indiana: Indiana University Press, 2002), 100.

[31] Jennifer A. Clack, *Gaining Ground: The Origin and Evolution of Tetrapods* (Indiana: Indiana University Press, 2002), 100.

[32] Ibid., 101.

[33] McNamara, K., and P. Selden. 1993. Strangers on the shore. *New Scientist* 139: 23-27. Quoted in Jennifer A. Clack, *Gaining Ground: The Origin and Evolution of Tetrapods* (Indiana: Indiana University Press, 2002), 104.

[34] Jennifer A. Clack, *Gaining Ground: The Origin and Evolution of Tetrapods* (Indiana: Indiana University Press, 2002), 104.

[35] Ibid., 175.

[36] Ibid., 176.

[37] Long, J.A. 1993. Cranial ribs in Devonian Lungfish and the origin of dipnoan air-breathing. *Memoirs of the Association of Australasian Palaeontologists* 15: 199-209.

Quoted in Jennifer A. Clack, *Gaining Ground: The Origin and Evolution of Tetrapods* (Indiana: Indiana University Press, 2002), 58.

[38] Jennifer A. Clack, *Gaining Ground: The Origin and Evolution of Tetrapods* (Indiana: Indiana University Press, 2002), 175.

[39] Ibid., 176.

[40] Ibid., 58.

[41] Ibid.

[42] Ibid.

[43] Long, J.A. 1993. Cranial ribs in Devonian Lungfish and the origin of dipnoan air-breathing. *Memoirs of the Association of Australasian Palaeontologists* 15: 199-209. Quoted in Jennifer A. Clack, *Gaining Ground: The Origin and Evolution of Tetrapods* (Indiana: Indiana University Press, 2002), 58.

[44] Panchen, A.L., and T.R. Smithson. 1987. Character diagnosis, fossils, and the origin of tetrapods. *Biological Reviews* 62: 341-438. Quoted in Jennifer A. Clack, *Gaining Ground: The Origin and Evolution of Tetrapods* (Indiana: Indiana University Press, 2002), 73.

[45] L. Grenade, 'Les Singularitéz de Londres, 1576', in Ann Saunders, *The Royal Exchange* (London: London Topographical Society, 1997), p. 48. Quoted in Markman Ellis, *The Coffee House: A Cultural History* (London: Weidenfeld & Nicolson, 2004), 166.

[46] Ned Ward, *The London-Spy Compleat, in Eighteen Parts,* 2nd ed. (London: J. How, 1704), p. 66. Quoted in Markman Ellis, *The Coffee House: A Cultural History* (London: Weidenfeld & Nicolson, 2004), 166.

[47] 'A Perticular of Writeings [on] the two houses in Exchange Alley', *c.* 1700, Appendix F. in John Martin, *'The Grasshopper' in Lombard Street* (London: Leadenhall Press, 1892), p. 299. Quoted in Markman Ellis, *The Coffee House: A Cultural History* (London: Weidenfeld & Nicolson, 2004), 167.

[48] *Kingdom's Intelligencer*, no. 51, 15-22 December 1662, p. 815. Quoted in Markman Ellis, *The Coffee House: A Cultural History* (London: Weidenfeld & Nicolson, 2004), 167.

[49] Ibid.

[50] Ibid.

[51] Ibid. Quoted in Markman Ellis, *The Coffee House: A Cultural History* (London: Weidenfeld & Nicolson, 2004), 168.

[52] Ibid. Quoted in Markman Ellis, *The Coffee House: A Cultural History* (London: Weidenfeld & Nicolson, 2004), 167.

[53] *Mercurius Publicus*, no. 49, 4-11 December 1662, p. 802. Quoted in Markman Ellis, *The Coffee House: A Cultural History* (London: Weidenfeld & Nicolson, 2004), 168.

[54] Pepys, *Diary*, I, p. 284; III, pp. 185-6. Quoted in Markman Ellis, *The Coffee House: A Cultural History* (London: Weidenfeld & Nicolson, 2004), 170.

[55] BL Add Mss 5100 (55*, fol. 166r-v); PRO, E 179/252/32 (3), p. 2 (R). Quoted in Markman Ellis, *The Coffee House: A Cultural History* (London: Weidenfeld & Nicolson, 2004), 168.

[56] Markman Ellis, *The Coffee House: A Cultural History* (London: Weidenfeld & Nicolson, 2004), 168.

[57] *Mercurius Politicus*, no. 435, 23 September 1658, p. 887. Quoted in Markman Ellis, *The Coffee House: A Cultural History* (London: Weidenfeld & Nicolson, 2004), 168.

[58] Lorna Weatherill, *Consumer Behavior and Material Culture in Britain, 1660-1760* (London: Routledge, 1988), p. 157. Quoted in Markman Ellis, *The Coffee House: A Cultural History* (London: Weidenfeld & Nicolson, 2004), 168.

[59] *Particulars and Conditions of Sale, of all that Plantation, or Freehold Estate, called Studley-Park, situate In the Parish of Saint George, in the Island of Tobago; [...] together with the Negroes, Stock, and Utensils, hereafter mentioned; Which will be Sold by Auction, By Messrs, Young and Brooks, On Thursday the 30*[th] *of September, inst. 1773; At Garraway's Coffee-House, Exchange Alley, at One o'Clock in the Afternoon ([London]: n.p., n.d. [1773])*. Quoted in Markman Ellis, *The Coffee House: A Cultural History* (London: Weidenfeld & Nicolson, 2004), 170.

[60] John Houghton, *A Collection for Improvement of Husbandry and Trade*, 2 (6 April 1692), p. [I]. Quoted in Markman Ellis,

The Coffee House: A Cultural History (London: Weidenfeld & Nicolson, 2004), 173.

⁶¹ John McCusker, 'European Bills of Entry and Marine Lists', *Harvard Library Bulletin*, 31: 3 (1983), pp. 209-55; 31: 4 (1983), pp. 316-39, pp. 316-26. Quoted in Markman Ellis, *The Coffee House: A Cultural History* (London: Weidenfeld & Nicolson, 2004), 173.

⁶² Ibid. Quoted in Markman Ellis, *The Coffee House: A Cultural History* (London: Weidenfeld & Nicolson, 2004), 173-174.

⁶³ *The Spectator*, no. 46, 23 April, 1711, ed. Bond, I, p. 196. Quoted in Markman Ellis, *The Coffee House: A Cultural History* (London: Weidenfeld & Nicolson, 2004), 178.

⁶⁴ Markman Ellis, *The Coffee House: A Cultural History* (London: Weidenfeld & Nicolson, 2004), 178.

⁶⁵ Ibid.

⁶⁶ Michie, *Stock Exchange*, pp. 19-20. Quoted in Markman Ellis, *The Coffee House: A Cultural History* (London: Weidenfeld & Nicolson, 2004), 174.

⁶⁷ Ibid.

⁶⁸ Ibid.

⁶⁹ Ibid.

⁷⁰ Ibid.

⁷¹ Markman Ellis, *The Coffee House: A Cultural History* (London: Weidenfeld & Nicolson, 2004), 174.

⁷² Mortimer, *Every Man his Own Broker*, p. 72n. Quoted in Markman Ellis, *The Coffee House: A Cultural History* (London: Weidenfeld & Nicolson, 2004), 179.

⁷³ S.R. Cope, 'The Stock-Brokers find a home: how the Stock Exchange came to be established in Sweetings Alley in 1773', *Guildhall Studies in London History*, II: 4 (April 1977), pp. 213-19. See also Dickson, *Financial Revolution*, pp. 490-

505. Quoted in Markman Ellis, *The Coffee House: A Cultural History* (London: Weidenfeld & Nicolson, 2004), 179.

[74] Cope, 'Stock-Brokers', p. 217. Quoted in Markman Ellis, *The Coffee House: A Cultural History* (London: Weidenfeld & Nicolson, 2004), 180.

[75] Ibid.

[76] *The Morning Chronicle*, no. 1291, 13 July 1773, p. [3]. Quoted in Markman Ellis, *The Coffee House: A Cultural History* (London: Weidenfeld & Nicolson, 2004), 180.

[77] Markman Ellis, *The Coffee House: A Cultural History* (London: Weidenfeld & Nicolson, 2004), 179.

[78] Bayles, p. 128. Quoted in Markman Ellis, *The Coffee House: A Cultural History* (London: Weidenfeld & Nicolson, 2004), 180.

[79] Ibid.

[80] Bayles, quoted p. 278. Quoted in Markman Ellis, *The Coffee House: A Cultural History* (London: Weidenfeld & Nicolson, 2004), 181.

[81] Markman Ellis, *The Coffee House: A Cultural History* (London: Weidenfeld & Nicolson, 2004), 181-182.

[82] Ibid., 182.

[83] Ibid.

[84] Henry W. Domett, *A History of the Bank of New York*, 2nd ed. (G.P. Putnam's Sons, 1884), pp. 7-15. Quoted in Markman Ellis, *The Coffee House: A Cultural History* (London: Weidenfeld & Nicolson, 2004), 182.

[85] Ibid.

[86] Markman Ellis, *The Coffee House: A Cultural History* (London: Weidenfeld & Nicolson, 2004), 182.

[87] Madison to Jefferson, 10 July 1791, *The Republic of Letters: The Correspondence between Thomas Jefferson and James Madison 1776-1826,* ed. James Morton Smith, 3 vols (New York: W.W. Norton, 1995), p. 696. Quoted in Markman Ellis,

The Coffee House: A Cultural History (London: Weidenfeld & Nicolson, 2004), 182.

[88] Ibid.

[89] Ibid.

[90] Ibid., 183.

[91] Markman Ellis, *The Coffee House: A Cultural History* (London: Weidenfeld & Nicolson, 2004), 183.

[92] Edmund Stedman and Alexander Easton, 'The History of the New York Stock Exchange' in *The New Stock Exchange*, ed. Edmund Stedman (New York: Stock Exchange Historical Co., 1905), pp. 17-43; Peter Eisenstadt, 'How the Buttonwood Tree Grew: the Making of a New York Stock Exchange Legend', *Prospects: An Annual of American Cultural Studies*, 19 (1994), pp. 75-98. Quoted in Markman Ellis, *The Coffee House: A Cultural History* (London: Weidenfeld & Nicolson, 2004), 183.

[93] Kenneth Jackson (ed.), *The Encyclopedia of New York* (New Haven, Conn.: Yale University Press, 1995) Quoted in Markman Ellis, *The Coffee House: A Cultural History* (London: Weidenfeld & Nicolson, 2004), 183.

[94] Ibid.

[95] The NYSEB changed its name to the New York Stock Exchange prior to finding a final location. However, we will make absolute use of the acronym NYSEB for the purposes of this analysis.

[96] "History of Flight," National Aeronautics and Space Administration (NASA): Ultra-Efficient Engine Technology Program, http://www.ueet.nasa.gov/ StudentSite/historyofflight.html.

[97] "History of Astronomy," MSN Encarta, http:// encarta.msn.com/encnet/refpages/RefArticle. aspx?refid=761572208.

[98] This assumes that each and every unemployed person

actually wants to work and is actively seeking employment. This also assumes that an adequate number of jobs exist. [99] This notion assumes that Osama bin Laden is still alive.

Sources

Clack, Jennifer A. *Gaining Ground: The Origin and Evolution of Tetrapods*. Bloomfield, Indiana: Indiana University Press, 2004.

Ellis, Markman. *The Coffee House: A Cultural History*. London: Weidenfeld & Nicolson, 2004.

MSN Encarta. "History of Astronomy," http://encarta.msn.com/encnet/refpages/RefArticle.aspx?refid=761572208 (accessed April 30, 2007).

National Aeronautics and Space Administration (NASA): Ultra-Efficient Engine Technology Program. "History of Flight," http://www.ueet.nasa.gov/StudentSite/historyofflight.html (accessed April 30, 2007).

Pegram, Thomas R. *Battling Demon Rum: The Struggle for a Dry America, 1800-1933*. Chicago: Ivan R. Dee, 1998.

U.S. National Archives and Records Administration, The. "Constitution of the United States: Amendments 11-27," http://www.archives.gov/national-archives-experience/charters/constitution_amendments_11-27.html (accessed April 10, 2007).

Index

Made in the USA